Geoffrey Chaucer

Steve Ellis

Northcote House

in association with
The British Council

© Copyright 1996 by Steve Ellis

First published in 1996 by Northcote House Publishers Ltd, Plymbridge House, Estover Road, Plymouth PL6 7PZ, United Kingdom.
Tel: +44 (0) 1752 202300. Fax: +44 (0) 1752 202330.

British Library Cataloguing-in-Publication Data
A catalogue record for this book is available from the British Library

ISBN 0 7463 0777 2

Typeset by PDQ Typesetting, Newcastle-Under-Lyme
Printed and bound in the United Kingdom

To Maureen, Suzanne, and Valerie,
fellow Birmingham Chaucerians

Contents

Acknowledgements

I should particularly like to thank Valerie Edden, who is more responsible than anyone for keeping me 'at' Chaucer, and Suzanne Reynolds, both of whom have commented helpfully on an earlier draft of this book. And to the succession of undergraduate students who have taken Chaucer classes with me, and to those students who have taken the MA in Chaucer Studies at Birmingham, I am deeply grateful. I should also like to thank Isobel Armstrong, Brian Hulme, and Hilary Walford for their help in the preparation of the typescript.

Biographical Outline

Early 1340s	Chaucer born, probably in London.
1357	Page in the household of the Countess of Ulster.
1359–60	Captured during wars in France and ransomed by the Crown.
1360s	*Valettus* and esquire to Edward III.
1366	Diplomatic mission to Spain.
By 1366	Marriage to Philippa Chaucer.
1367	Receives life annuity from Edward III.
1368 or 1369	Blanche, Duchess of Lancaster, wife of John of Gaunt, dies. Chaucer writes the *Book of the Duchess*.
1372–3	First mission on Crown business to Italy.
1374–86	Controller of customs in the port of London.
1374–c.1386	Holds lease on dwelling over city gate at Aldgate.
1378	Second mission to Italy.
c.1378	*House of Fame* written.
1380	Cecily Chaumpaigne's release to Chaucer concerning her *raptus*.
1380	Lewis Chaucer born.
c.1380	*Parliament of Fowls* written.
c.1385	*Troilus and Criseyde* and *Boece* finished.
1385–9	Justice of the Peace for Kent.
1386	Testifies, at age of 'forty years and more', in legal case involving the Scrope family.
1386	MP for county of Kent.
c.1386	*Legend of Good Women* written.
By 1387	Philippa Chaucer dies.
c.1386–1400	*Canterbury Tales* written.
1389–91	Clerk of the King's Works.
1390	Robbed three times between 3 and 6 September.

c.1391	*Treatise on the Astrolabe* written.
1394	Granted royal annuity of £20.
1399	Further annuity from Henry IV.
1399	Takes lease on a house in grounds of Westminster Abbey.
1400	Dies in London. Buried in what has since become Poets' Corner, Westminster Abbey.

A Note on the Text

All quotations from Chaucer are taken from *The Riverside Chaucer*, ed. L. D. Benson *et al.* (3rd edn., Oxford, 1988). A Glossary listing the modern meanings for Middle English terms in the Chaucer quotations used in this work is included at the end of this book.

Introduction:
The Chaucer Business

'They met in a pub. Got very very merry. They started telling tales. Lechery, treachery, that sort of thing. Free nosh for the best story.' Thus the cover of the *Radio Times* for 16 October 1969, advertising a new television production of the *Canterbury Tales* that started transmission the following week. The adapters, Martin Starkie and Nevill Coghill, had recently provided framework and text (based on Coghill's well-known translation, 1951) for a highly successful musical of the *Tales* that ran for several years in London's West End and that today still frequently tours in Britain and the USA. Vying with this in its share of the popular Chaucer market is the Phil Woods/Michael Bogdanov adaptation of the *Tales*, again a familiar item in the modern theatre repertoire and, in the words of the *Time Out* review of the first production, an 'ebullient romp...dull it ain't' (19 January 1979). The idea of Chaucer as adult pantomime and of the *Tales* as a kind of pub-outing also underlay the BBC Radio 4 transmission of several (again much adapted) tales in March–April 1991, stories accompanied by plentiful guffawing, thigh-slapping and ale-slurping on the part of their narrators.

Perhaps with no other author is the gulf between the popular and academic reception so marked. While Chaucer carouses his way through theatres and the media in this country and abroad, Chaucer scholars continue their earnest proliferation of books and articles that also have a world-wide audience, notably in Europe, the USA, and the Far East. Far from a simple, merry Chaucer infused with a dose of late-1960s liberationism that stage and screen purvey, the academic Chaucer industry has evolved a formidably complex, contradictory, and unfinalized author of

1

whom, as A. C. Spearing remarked in his short study of *Troilus and Criseyde*, 'almost no interpretative statement can be made...that does not require correction by its opposite'.[1] Chaucer scholars themselves have occasionally been known to worry about the academic appropriation of Chaucer, and about the fact that an educated but non-professional readership for his work that might fill the gap between the popular and academic reception seems to be relatively lacking.[2] This gap was prominent by the end of the 1960s with *Canterbury Tales – The Musical*, on the one hand, and, on the other, the school of patristic Chaucerian exegesis pioneered by D. W. Robertson, Jr., which enjoyed a prestigious position within the academy. In books like *A Preface to Chaucer* (1962), and *Fruyt and Chaf: Studies in Chaucer's Allegories* (1963) (co-written with B. F. Huppé), Robertson discounted any modern reception of Chaucer by insisting that his works, like all medieval literature, were written to promote Christian charity at the expense of cupidity, a distinction laid down in St Augustine's *De doctrina Christiana*, and that where this aim is not apparent the reader must learn to uncover the essential meaning beneath the veil of the letter. Armed with a formidable knowledge of medieval biblical commentary, Robertson developed a series of readings of Chaucer's works that brought out their supposed Christian orthodoxy, often enshrined within a whole system of arcane allegory. Thus the Wife of Bath should be viewed not as a picture of lovable bawdiness but as an exponent of consistent exegetical misinterpretation in the way she understands biblical and patristic texts, marking her as preferring 'the law of fallen nature to the law of grace'.[3] And, of course, one can only know how widely she misinterprets by knowing the Church Fathers, and through them the correct interpretation, thoroughly.

Even though much modern Chaucer scholarship has concentrated on retrieving medieval cultural/political contexts in which his work is to be understood, and so separating the specialist from the general reader, one might hazard the generalization that before the 1960s this separation had yet to become marked. The eminent Harvard professor George Kittredge published his well-known *Chaucer and his Poetry* in 1915, a book that was influential in its attempt to bring Chaucer to the modern reader by seeing his work as primarily a study in unchanging human nature – 'mankind as it was, and is'[4] – and the *Tales* as a set of soliloquies delivered by the dramatis personae of the 'General Prologue'. What one needed to understand Chaucer was not a knowledge of the Middle Ages but a sympathy with 'life' itself in all its variety, and the recognition that Chaucer's main bent was for the multiple characterization that the Shakespearian drama and modern novel would develop. Many academics continued to stress this fundamental idea of Chaucer as the celebrant of human nature even when bringing other contexts to him; as Nevill Coghill, my Writers and their Work predecessor, put it in his 1956 contribution to the series, Chaucer 'is all things to all men and women'.[5] One of the many problems with this assumption was the tendency to see the rest of Chaucer's work as merely prefatory to the Tales, or even as alien to his true vocation as the voice of 'Merrie England'. The reader fresh to Chaucer should be reminded that the Tales are only a portion of his œuvre, and that the heresy that sees them as not the most interesting portion of his work is not totally unknown.

Whereas Robertson and his school claimed to possess a 'key' that would unlock the definitive meaning of Chaucer's work, the scholarship of the last three decades has been much more sceptical that any such key exists. I quoted Spearing above on the need to see Chaucer as a set of mutually correcting oppositions, but this stance can itself become formulaic, and several books from the 1970s will promote Chaucer's complexity (or ability to see, and support, opposing positions at once) as a proto-modern tolerance and liberalism; Chaucer is varied, contradictory, ironic, and so on because 'truth' is too, an argument that can close down discussion of the texts as effectively (if more flexibly) as any Robertsonian critique. A classic example of this comfortable oppositionalism is Peter Elbow's Oppositions in Chaucer (1975). That such oppositions are there, but as expressions of different social, cultural, and gendered voices in vigorous and unresolved conflict, is perhaps the major emphasis of Chaucer criticism produced in the 1980s and 1990s. One of the best-known recent books, Paul Strohm's Social Chaucer (1989), is from an author who declares his solidarity 'with those critics who assert the possibility of unresolved contention, of a struggle between hegemony and counter-hegemony, of texts as places crowded with many voices representing many centers of social authority'.[6] Chaucer's work is the site of a particularly active contention, between, for example, different social classes and different models of social organization, given the transition Chaucer records from the hierarchical 'three-estates' model of society to the emerging world of urban, mercantile capital handily summarized by David Aers in his 1986 book on Chaucer; between the voices of women and the power of patriarchy invested in the Church, the system of government, the marriage market, and the institution of literature itself; and between the differing world-views traced in the work of Mikhail Bakhtin – that is, the contention between a 'laughing', carnivalesque view of reality and the official ideology of seriousness that this aims to subvert. Bakhtin's work has increasingly been drawn on by Chaucer scholars since the mid-1970s (as it has been by literary scholars working in several different fields), and, though it may be new to many readers of this book, it offers an interesting approach to works like the 'Miller's Tale' and the 'Wife of Bath's Prologue', as Chapters 5 and 6 will indicate. Bakhtin's discussion of polyphonic or 'multi-voiced' literature also underwrites the analysis of the *Canterbury Tales* as a contention between voices touched on above and returned to in Chapter 7.

Work informed by feminist interests and theory has also been an ever-increasing feature of Chaucer scholarship in recent years, and will often figure in this book, where I shall be concentrating on questions such as whether Chaucer's works promote or contest medieval anti-feminism; what value they place on human sexuality, as opposed to rationality and spirituality; how they relate to the literary tradition Chaucer inherited and the role of the poet passed down by his models; and what evidence they show of Chaucer as a political and social thinker. I should add that, in a book as short as this, it is impossible to discuss all of Chaucer's works, or even each of the *Tales*, in depth, and that various readers will regret some omissions, especially since I want to give due attention to the pre-*Tales* works for reasons touched on above. I also wish to examine several tropes that have always invested Chaucer's role, such as his being the 'Father of English Poetry' or the voice of 'Merrie England' and so forth, identities that readers new to Chaucer may still find lying in their path as they approach him.

Meanwhile the Chaucer business (show and academic) rolls on. This Introduction was first drafted in the summer of 1994 on the eve of the New Chaucer Society's International Congress, the major forum for Chaucer scholars, which that year was held in Dublin. A glance at the programme will illustrate as well as anything the present state of Chaucer studies. The conference was attended by several hundred delegates and offered over its four days practically as many papers, in sessions ranging from Feminist Chaucer Studies to The Study of Chaucerian Manuscripts, from Chaucer and Japanese Classical Literature to Chaucer and Spain, from Queer Chaucer to Chaucer and Chess. The Society's yearbook, *Studies in the Age of Chaucer*, listed in its 1994 volume over 300 books and articles on Chaucer or his immediate contexts that comprised the bibliography for the year 1992 alone. Although there were nearly twice as many items on the *Canterbury Tales* as on Chaucer's other works, it is clear that we are a long way from the simple Chaucer of popular merriment with whom we started. Today, Chaucer is truly a 'global' author, both in his following and in the variety of interests his work encompasses and generates, and it is this plurality that attends Chaucer studies that captures and excites students new to him every year who were expecting, perhaps, to have to endure a series of classes on medieval philology alone. Questions of gender and society, and of the status and signifying practices of the literary text itself, speak to us from Chaucer's texts and address some of our own most serious concerns.

1

Life, Works, Reputation

We do not know exactly where or when Chaucer was born (though London seems a safe answer to the first question), and indeed all biographies of him have to make do with a limited and by now rather stale set of facts around which a narrative can be woven; accounts of the 'Age of Chaucer' type abound, however, in which any shortfall in details relating to the author can be made up by lavish accounts of the court of Edward III. In giving evidence to a legal inquiry in 1386 Chaucer is recorded as being 'of forty years and more', and scholars generally accept a date of birth for him of some time in the early 1340s. His family, who originally came from East Anglia, had been settled for some time before his birth in the Vintry ward of the City of London, where his father indeed had a vintner's business, a circumstance that in some of the more picturesque novelizations of Chaucer's life has the infant poet already gathering material for the *Canterbury Tales* from the colourful and jovial characters pressing into his father's pub. His father, of course, was not an innkeeper but a wine merchant, a member of an affluent and influential mercantile class, and someone whose services to the Crown helped prepare the way for his son's entry into the royal household. We know nothing about Chaucer's education, though his court training doubtless fostered that love of reading he refers to throughout his works (notably in the *House of Fame* ll. 652–60), and the omnivorous intellectual interests they evince.

Nearly 500 documentary life-records relating to Chaucer survive from the Middle Ages, preserved in the invaluable compilation by Crow and Olson, and ranging from pleas of debt against Chaucer in the Court of Common Pleas to payments to him from the royal purse and court-records concerning three robberies he was subject to between 3 and 6 September 1390.

There are no records, however, relating to his infancy or boyhood, and our first account of him comes in 1357, when, as a page in the household of the Countess of Ulster, wife of Edward III's son Prince Lionel, he is in a list of those authorized to receive a new suit of clothes. The surviving document, reused as part of the binding for a medieval manuscript, was discovered in the late nineteenth century when an energetic trawling of royal, civic, and legal records was conducted in search of Chaucer, inspired by the indefatigable F. J. Furnivall, who set up (along with much else) the Chaucer Society in 1868. The other best-known early document relates to the ransom payment of £16 paid by the Crown to secure the release of Chaucer, captured in France during Edward III's campaign against the French in 1359–60.

We do not know precisely how someone born into a mercantile background came to enter and serve in court circles, and the records from the first twenty-five years of Chaucer's life are far too scanty to serve us. Speculation and hearsay have always flourished in the 'gaps' of Chaucer's life, and at various times he has been enrolled as a student at Oxford or Cambridge (or both), and in the Inns of Court, but all this is conjectural and highly unlikely. By the 1360s, however, Chaucer had transferred to the household of the king himself, and records of payments to him as *valettus* and esquire to Edward III exist from 1367 for the next ten years. In the words of his most recent biographer, Derek Pearsall, Chaucer's life would be tied, 'like that of a page', to 'the daily rhythms of feasting, sport, practice in the martial arts, hunting, music, dancing and song, and to the annual cycle of festivals, visits and campaigns'; there would also be various administrative and diplomatic tasks to fill out the duties of the squires, who were a 'kind of lay secretariat'.[1] In between these duties Chaucer found time to write his first major poem, the elegy for Blanche, Duchess of Lancaster, wife of Edward III's third surviving son, John of Gaunt, usually known as the *Book of the Duchess*, and generally accepted as dating from soon after her death, which took place in 1368 or 1369.

One traditional categorization of Chaucer's works has been to divide them into three periods, an early French period covering the *Book of the Duchess* and the translation of the *Romance of the Rose* (which we know from Chaucer's own evidence in a later poem that he produced but which is probably not the surviving middle-English fragment printed in Chaucer's *Works*); a middle Italian period covering the 1370s and first half of the 1380s, when Chaucer's writings drew extensively on the work of Dante and Boccaccio; and a final English period, synonymous with the *Canterbury Tales*. This periodization is, however, very difficult to justify. It is true that the *Book of the Duchess* shows extensive borrowings from French 'dream-vision' literature, notably Machaut's *Jugement dou Roy de Behaingne* (*Judgement of the King of Bohemia*), and that in the chamber where the dreamer wakes 'alle the walles with colours fyne I Were peynted, bothe text and glose, I Of al the Romaunce of the Rose' (ll. 332–4), but the *Romance of the Rose* remains a powerful presence in Chaucer's poetry up into the *Tales* themselves, where it informs, for example, the portrayal of the Wife of Bath and the debating strategies in her 'Prologue'. Similarly, although the *Book of the Duchess* does predate Chaucer's interest in Italian poetry, that interest, once aroused in the 1370s, stays with Chaucer throughout his life and is again evident in the *Tales*. That the *Tales*, regarded as the consummation of Chaucer's life's work, have been seen as representative of an 'English period' says less about their deriving from a native line of literature (though Chaucer does draw on English folk-tales and romances in some of them) than the belief that here Chaucer went beyond literary models altogether (especially 'foreign' ones) and directly transcribed the 'real life' all around him, in a peculiarly vivid, national form. Thus many nineteenth- and twentieth-century writers on Chaucer saw the *Tales* and their 'Prologue' as a paean to the robustness and individuality of the national character, with figures like the Host, Harry Bailly, and the Wife of Bath modelling this supremely. I shall return in my final chapter to the ways in which Chaucer has been requisitioned for a nationalist ideology, but I should point out here that often where 'life' seems at its most intense in the *Tales* Chaucer is drawing on his reading and working intertextually: I have alluded to the features from the *Romance of the Rose* (the depiction of the Old Woman in Book 7) that are reused in the Wife of Bath, and from the same source comes the celebrated picture of the Prioress's table manners in the 'General Prologue' (ll. 127–36; compare the *Romance*, l. 13355 ff.), not from a woman observed eating in the Tabard Inn. More generally, the celebrated realism of several tales is inspired by their sources in French fabliaux, and it is a moot point how far Chaucer's abilities in characterization and dialogue were prompted by his reading of Dante's *Divine Comedy*. As Mario Praz once remarked (though with a different emphasis), Chaucer may have had to go to Italy to learn how to depict the English.[2] And we must also remember how far Chaucer's work is steeped in classical literature, especially Virgil and Ovid, and in later writers like Boethius, Macrobius, and so on.

We know that Chaucer made two trips to Italy in the 1370s, the first to Genoa and Florence between December 1372 and May 1373 and the second to Lombardy in 1378. Both were on royal business, the first primarily to treat with the Genoese about their use of English seaports (and possibly, in Florence, to deal with the Bardi family, Edward III's bankers) and the second to conduct undisclosed negotiations relating to the war with France. We cannot know whether he met Petrarch or Boccaccio on that first trip, but there is no doubting the interest Chaucer takes in Italian literature from this time, as noted above. In 1374 Chaucer received his best-known appointment, that of customs controller in the port of London, a post he was to occupy for over twelve years. His job was basically to oversee the collectors of tolls in their work and vet their accounts, representing the royal interest as beneficiary of the customs duty; he remained a member of the royal household, and when he was on other business (such as the Lombardy mission above) a deputy controller was appointed.

These were without doubt very busy years for Chaucer, and a glance at the Crow and Olson life-records covering the controller-ship indicates the volume and intricacy of work passing through his hands. The demands of combining this with a literary vocation are amusingly set out by him in the *House of Fame*:

> For when thy labour doon al ys,
> And hast mad alle thy rekenynges,
> In stede of reste and newe thynges
> Thou goost hom to thy hous anoon,
> And, also domb as any stoon,
> Thou sittest at another book
> Tyl fully daswed ys thy look...

(ll. 652–8)

It is, of course, this ability to combine the roles of man of business, diplomat, and poet that has endeared Chaucer to many modern commentators searching for a model of the 'well-rounded' man. The idea of Chaucer as a man of the world, plentifully endowed with practical wisdom and the sense of civic duty, is foremost in many non-academic appreciations of him written in the last 200 years, often to expose by contrast (implicitly or openly) a current 'anti-social' or bohemian 'model' of the poet. Moreover, as 'Something in the City' in G. K. Chesterton's phrase, Chaucer has often appealed to a supposed English taste for poets who shall not be too suspiciously 'poetic', who shall not only write for the 'ordinary man' but even embody him as he goes about his nine-to-five business.[3] With the 1960s, as I remarked at the outset of this book, the popular image of Chaucer may be said to have become rather less respectable. The sexual freedoms that had previously to be apologized for now mark Chaucer's work as progressive.

The major literary works that derive from Chaucer's controllership years (though we have no way of dating them exactly) are two further poems in dream-vision form, the *House of Fame* and the *Parliament of Fowls*, and his long, self-declared 'tragic' poem *Troilus and Criseyde*, the two last being written in the first half of the 1380s. He also produced a prose translation of Boethius's *Consolation of Philosophy* (the *Boece*), a work that has crucial bearings on *Troilus*. In the *Legend of Good Women*, a poem written in the mid-1380s as an 'apology' for the supposed defamation of Criseyde in the previous poem, Chaucer gives a list of his own works to date in the 'Prologue' (which exists in two versions, labelled 'F' and 'G'). Apart from the writings mentioned thus far we are told of some translations of devotional works (now lost) and 'al the love of Palamon and Arcite | Of Thebes' and 'the lyf... of Seynt Cecile' (G version, ll. 408–16), two poems that enter the *Canterbury Tales* as the 'Knight's Tale' and 'Second Nun's Tale'. Thus, although Chaucer's most famous work is generally ascribed to the remaining years of his life from the late 1380s to the traditional date of his death (25 October 1400), it is clear that he reused some earlier material. The 'Prologue' to the *Legend* also tells us that Chaucer wrote 'many an ympne for [Love's] halydayes, | That highten balades, roundeles, vyrelayes' (ll. 410–11), and, although many of these have been lost, the surviving 'short poems', twenty-one in number, include one roundel, 'Merciles Beaute', and several 'balades'. There is a further unfinished poem, *Anelida and Arcite*, and the prose *Treatise on the Astrolabe*, which Chaucer wrote, as he says at the start of the work, for the instruction on that instrument of 'Lyte [little] Lowys my son' in his 'tendir age of ten yeer', and which probably dates, on internal evidence, to 1391.

In referring to this last work (which is essentially a compilation from earlier Arabic astronomers) Pearsall in his recent biography notes that

> Chaucer, as usual, without making much fuss about it, and in a manner workmanlike rather than supremely accomplished, seems to have come close to inventing English scientific prose, just as he had invented the pentameter, the pentameter couplet and rhyme royal [during the 1380s, in the *Anelida, Parliament, Troilus*, and *Legend*], and done the first English prose translation since Anglo-Saxon times of a major Latin philosophical work, in his *Boece*.[4]

If we can hardly begrudge Chaucer his traditional title of 'Father of English Poetry', we need to be aware of the nationalist-patriarchal implications of such a title, as summarized in my concluding chapter. In the meantime, we have the picture of a busy public man, with interests that encompassed the arts and science of his day, and one withal, in Pearsall's comment, who saw nothing unusual or exceptional in this range, not being able to look back nostalgically at himself from the specialization of twentieth-century intellectual life: the parallel with Dante is obvious, even though the latter's multifarious interests and activities have tended to eclipse Chaucer's, partly because Dante never had to put up with the image of the jolly toper that Chaucer has been saddled with by future ages.

It seems that Chaucer had married his wife, Philippa, a member of the household of Edward III's queen (also Philippa), by 1366, and that, after the queen's death in 1369, Philippa Chaucer moved to John of Gaunt's household, attending on his second wife, Constance of Castile. The claim arising in the sixteenth century that Philippa was the sister of Katherine de Roet, who became John of Gaunt's third wife in 1396, is generally accepted, though not proven. Records of rather irregular annuity payments to Philippa for her services in the royal household cease in 1387, suggesting her death in that year. The *Treatise on the Astrolabe* indicates that the couple had at least one son, Lewis, born in 1380, though separate documents exist that mention a Thomas and an Elizabeth Chaucer, who may be further offspring. On 29 November 1873 the *Athenaeum* magazine reported the discovery of a new and sensational document concerning Chaucer, the enrolment in Chancery in 1380 of a release by one Cecily Chaumpaigne to him, freeing him of all legal actions concerning her *raptus*.[5] This tantalizing discovery has occasioned vigorous debate: did 'raptus' signify rape, seduction, or abduction on someone else's behalf; was Chaucer a principal or accessory in the affair, and so forth. Furnivall, one of the first to discuss the case in one of his Chaucer Society publications, while 'wish[ing] this record...had not been on the Close Roll', took a lenient view:

> I think it certain that Chaucer committed no felony... yet there must remain the possibility that he lay with [Cecily], and compensated her... if we take the worst possible view of it – violent rape not being possible – it only shows that a thing happened, which any one from certain of Chaucer's Tales, must have known might well have happened, and which was hardly considered a fault in the gentleman of his day.[6]

Others have felt less certain that the action exemplifies Chaucer's gentlemanly status, however, and some historians who have investigated the case in depth, such as P. R. Watts, have concluded that the act was one of rape, a charge supported by the discovery of a recent document by Christopher Cannon.[7] Other speculations include the idea that Cecily was holding the threat of rape against Chaucer as leverage for some other injustice by him committed against her, and that one issue of the business was 'little Lewis' himself, 10 years old in 1391.

Chaucer was in trouble more than once in his later years, with legal actions against him for debt and trespass, as well as the Chaumpaigne case. He was also, however, a Justice of the Peace for Kent between 1385 and 1389 and an MP for the same county in 1386. Recent events remind us that parliamentary office and delinquency are not mutually exclusive, whether for the 1380s or 1980s. No records exist of any cases brought before Chaucer as JP, and we have more information concerning his next post, that as Clerk of the Works for Westminster, the Tower of London, and other royal buildings, during 1389–91. Here Chaucer was in overall control of purchasing and transporting materials for repairs and rebuilding, and recruiting and supervising the workforce. The major projects during his office were the construction of a new wool wharf by the Tower of London and the building of scaffolds in Smithfield for the jousts of May 1390. There was also some uncompleted work at St George's Chapel, Windsor.

Chaucer held other minor offices during the last decade of his life, but his staple income was the life annuity he had received for good service from Edward III in 1367, confirmed by Richard II shortly after his accession in 1378, renewed in 1394 at £20 after a period of surrender and supplemented by a further annuity of 40 Marks from Henry IV in 1399. Various other royal grants in the 1390s (including an annual tun of wine bestowed in 1397) secured the prosperity of Chaucer's later years, and in 1399 he took the lease on a house in the garden of the Lady Chapel of Westminster Abbey, and died the following year, on 25 October, according to the now illegible inscription on his tomb in the Abbey. Being buried there was no indication of celebrity: though Chaucer 'founded' Poets' Corner, the Abbey had recently become a regular burial place for royal officials and courtiers. Nor must we over-estimate Chaucer's importance in court circles; Pearsall has estimated Chaucer's household services as 'routine', and suggested that 'if Edward III or Richard II actually knew Chaucer it was with but a fleeting recognition'.[8] And there is no evidence that the not particularly bookish kings through whose reigns Chaucer lived were in any sense his literary patrons, despite the well-known pictorial fancy by Ford Madox Brown of *Chaucer Reading at the Court of Edward III* (in Sydney), a work deriving from the Corpus Christi frontispiece (see Chapter 4 below on Chaucer's audience).

Apart from the Westminster house, Chaucer's other documen-ted place of residence was a dwelling above the city gate of Aldgate, on which he took a lease in 1374 and which may have been held till 1386. The reader may have noticed that so far in this account of Chaucer's life little attention has been paid to contemporary political events, even though Chaucer had first-hand acquaintance with the French wars, the turbulent career and parliaments of Richard II, and the Peasants' Revolt of 1381. Indeed, it is a statutory feature of Chaucer biography to create the tableau of Chaucer in his house above Aldgate witnessing the rebels breaking through the gate into the city beneath him, as happened on the night of 12–13 June 1381; it has also become conventional to wonder at Chaucer's seeming indifference to the political turmoil around him, given the dearth of references to any of these events in the works themselves. In the penultimate chapter of this book I shall consider Chaucer in his political context, after an appraisal of the most important of these works; I shall end this chapter with some brief remarks on the history of the Chaucerian text, and on Chaucer's changing reputation in the light of this.

No manuscript of any of Chaucer's poems exists from his own hand, though the earliest copy of the *Tales*, the Hengwrt manuscript in the National Library of Wales, Aberystwyth, dates from soon after his death. The relative frequency of early fifteenth-century manuscripts of the *Tales*, together with the praises of Chaucer in the work of writers like Lydgate and Hoccleve, testify to Chaucer's immediate posthumous reputation; in his *Regement of Princes* (written 1411–12), Hoccleve refers to Chaucer as his 'mayster dere' and as 'flour of eloquence, | Mirrour of fructuous entendement [fruitful understanding], | ... universal fader in science!' (ll. 1961–4), and leaves us the nearest thing we have to Chaucer's portrait (reproduced as the frontispiece to this book). Towards the end of the fifteenth century Chaucer's work is fêted in the writings of the so-called Scottish Chaucerians, the best-known example being Robert Henryson's *Testament of Cresseid*, a continuation of *Troilus and Criseyde* 'writtin be [by] worthie Chaucer glorious' (l. 41). By this period the *Tales* had appeared in print, from William Caxton and others, but it was not until 1532 that the first printed version of the entire *Works* came out, edited by William Thynne, followed by the John Stow edition of 1561 and the two editions by Robert Speght of 1598 and 1602. The most celebrated sixteenth-century allusion to Chaucer is in canto II of the fourth book of Spenser's *Faerie Queene*, where Chaucer is the 'well of English undefyled' (stanza 32), but the host of references to him from this and subsequent periods can be examined in Caroline Spurgeon's massive compilation.[9] Sometimes these references are to spurious works which the early editions (and many later ones) included, such as the *Testament of Love* (actually by Thomas Usk), an ascription responsible for the repeated assertion that, as Leigh Hunt later enthused, 'Chaucer was four years in prison in his old age for the freedom of his opinions'.[10] Chaucer was also hailed as a political agitator (unlikely as it may seem) at the time of the Reformation, largely on the basis of the anti-Church invective of the 'Plowman's Tale', again thought to be his. It was Chaucer's great eighteenth-century editor Thomas

Tyrwhitt who cleared many of the bogus items from the Chaucer canon, though he still accepted poems like 'The Cuckoo and the Nightingale' and 'The Flower and the Leaf', the latter in particular enjoying great popularity in the nineteenth century from Wordsworth and Keats to Burne-Jones. Indeed, works he did not write have had at times a greater Chaucerian vogue than works he did.

It is generally agreed that the seventeenth century is the low point of Chaucer's fortunes, with no edition of his works appearing between 1602 and 1687. Complaints about the barbarity of Chaucer's style and diction are routine, and it is not until the publication of Dryden's *Fables* in 1700, with its celebrated and enthusiastic 'Preface' (which includes the famous phrases 'the Father of English Poetry' and, on the characters of the *Tales*, 'here is God's Plenty'), that we have a restoration of fortune. Dryden's book includes translations of several Tales, for 'Chaucer...is a rough Diamond, and must first be polish'd e'er he shines', thus setting the fashion for similar modernizations by many poets, including Pope and Wordsworth.[11] Tyrwhitt's five-volume edition of the *Tales* (1775–8) marks, as stated above, the emergence of the modern text, but one might say that the founding of modern scholarship on Chaucer is the work of the second half of the nineteenth century, led by the archival and textual labours of Furnivall and the Chaucer Society. This more responsible documentation is anticipated by biographers like Sir Harris Nicolas (compare the 'Life of Chaucer' prefixed to his edition of the *Romance of the Rose* (1846) with the diffuse and fanciful biography of William Godwin published in 1803), and by mid-century editors like Richard Morris, who looked freshly at manuscript sources.

Although Furnivall could still complain, in an article of 1873, of his age's 'pitiable indifference' to Chaucer,[12] there is no doubting the mounting interest shown in him during that century by scholars and *litterati* at least, as the work of writers like Keats, Scott, Leigh Hunt, Ruskin, and William Morris indicates. But a wider public interest had been forestalled in part by the absence of a reliable and authoritative text, a gap filled by the landmark Oxford edition of W. W. Skeat (1894–7) and the Student's Edition reprint of the text (1895). It would be impossible here to refer to all the important scholarship produced in England, Europe, and the

USA in the latter half of the century, but mention must be made of Lounsbury's magisterial *Studies in Chaucer* (1892), a book that is in some ways a consummation of that scholarship. Lounsbury himself traces the gradual emergence of a reliable text and a reliable biography, and insists on a reading of Chaucer as a sophisticated and sceptical man of letters rather than the jovial 'Dan Chaucer' figure still present in many nineteenth-century responses. On the eve of the twentieth century, then, Chaucer comes into his own, with a restored text, an accurate biography, and a set of up-to-date opinions; in short, something of a modernist, and more 'himself', in Lounsbury's eyes, than at any time since he actually lived and wrote. What twentieth-century scholars have made of this retrieved Chaucer will be considered during my discussions of the works themselves that follow.

A final word on the modern Chaucerian text. The standard edition today is the Oxford *Riverside Chaucer* (first published 1987), based on F. N. Robinson's second edition of the *Works* (1957), though some texts like the *Troilus* and the *Romance of the Rose* have been thoroughly revised. Robinson himself in revising his original 1933 edition drew on the Manly-Rickert edition of the *Tales* (1940), and, for the vexed questions that concern the proper order of the *Tales*, the best manuscript authority for them, and the possibility of a 'publication' of individual Tales in Chaucer's lifetime, students can consult the Introductions to these editions or N. F. Blake's 1985 study, *The Textual Tradition of the Canterbury Tales*. Many of Chaucer's individual poems have been published in separate editions, and it is needless to name them here, other perhaps than the important *Troilus and Criseyde* brought out by Barry Windeatt in 1984.

2

Dreams, Texts, Truth

Many of Chaucer's major works before the *Canterbury Tales* are written in the so-called 'dream-vision' form derived from French tradition, where, as in the *Romance of the Rose*, the narrator recounts his falling asleep and his subsequent dream, the subject of which is principally the pleasures and travails of love. Chaucer's dream-visions are nothing like the length of the *Rose*, of course, but, if we compare them with their shorter French sources, we see how Chaucer extends the form to cover weighty philosophical matters like mortality and consolation, the status of textual authority, and the place of human sexuality within the natural order. This thematic enriching is synonymous with the form being used to explore problems rather than reach conclusions; indeed, two of the dream-visions, the *House of Fame* and the *Legend of Good Women*, literally have no conclusion and the two that are finished, the *Book of the Duchess* and the *Parliament of Fowls*, have endings whose emphatic closures only point up the fact that no solution has been found to the questions posed.

This is apparent if we compare the *Book of the Duchess*, Chaucer's earliest 'major' poem, with its principal source, Machaut's *Judgement of the King of Bohemia*. Modern readers are often horrified at the discovery that the portrait of Blanche, Duchess of Lancaster (whose elegy this poem is), is based closely in some respects on the grieving knight's lady in the Machaut, as if the poem's 'sincerity' is thereby impugned, though it is always easier to spot the conventions governing earlier 'portraiture' (be they in medieval text or tomb effigy) than those governing our own. The Machaut poem is essentially a debate over whether a lover who suffers loss through the partner's death is in more pain than one who suffers through infidelity; at the end of the poem the two lovers put their cases to the king, who, guided by the allegorical figure of Reason among others, solves the problem by finding on behalf of the betrayed lover's greater pain, a verdict universally accepted. Everyone goes off, the lovers included, happy with the arbitration.

Chaucer's poem reaches no such acceptable conclusion. Though it is indebted to the Machaut for some of the portrait of Blanche, as well as for some details of plot and description, it reaches no clear or comforting 'verdict'. There is only one lover, of course, the 'man in blak', generally accepted as a representation of John of Gaunt, mourning his dead wife. The poem is, therefore, both elegy and tribute to Blanche and a study in the pathology of grief, with the man in black repeatedly calling for his own death; indeed, the elegiac memorialization of Blanche's virtues is a knife-edged consolation for the mourner, since in recreating these splendours he finds himself 'compulsively repeat[ing] the trauma of her loss', in the words of Maud Ellmann's stimulating Freudian reading of the poem.[1] Blanche is elaborately brought back to life to introduce a lengthy and lulling description of the lovers' happiness over 'ful many a yere' (l. 1296), and then, almost at the end, her death is 'repeated' suddenly, emphatically and brutally in the exchange between mourner and narrator: ' "Sir", quod I, "where is she now?" I . . . "She ys Ded!" "Nay!" "Yis, be my trouthe!" I "Is that youre los? Be God, hyt ys routhe!"' (ll. 1298–1310). Indeed, the poem might be said to revitalize death in all its power by restaging its sudden seizure of Blanche, not by simply restating it.

Much of the critical discussion of the poem has centred on what sort of 'consolation' it might afford, be it internally to the man in black and/or narrator, or to the external audience coming to terms with Blanche's loss. Such consolation has been located in the beauty of the natural world the poem celebrates, or in the memory of a golden-age love there recorded, or in the artwork itself, evidencing the triumphant aesthetic reprocessing of the brute fact of loss. Allegorical readings have been put forward that see the man in black's return to the 'long castel with walles white' at the end of the poem (l. 1318) as the entry into the Heavenly Jerusalem (the consolation of Christian salvation),[2] or as his 'resocialization' into the aristocratic order, in Stephen Knight's phrase, and thus as the symbolic cessation of grief.[3] Indeed, it is interesting to compare the Marxist sociology of Knight with allegorical Christian readings of the text to get some idea of the range of readings the poem elicits. But both these readings, and many others, suggest that Chaucer is still providing some sort of 'cure' for pathological grief, whereas I would argue that the poem's proper subject is one not of future consolation but of present impasse, a statement of problems that remain unresolved in this poem and that Chaucer himself 'compulsively repeats' in his later works. This reading is in line with the troubled and problematic Chaucer presented throughout this present book, in contrast to the genial celebrant of 'nature', 'love', or human personality often surmised. Chaucer is rather a poet of deadlock, as my readings of *Troilus* and the Wife of Bath will also show, even when the deadlock is disguised as resolution.

In the famous Wheel of Fortune image that governs *Troilus and Criseyde*, we find that the lovers' happiness is intensified by the sorrows they have been through, but that the pain of parting is in turn increased by that experience of happiness at its peak; when Troilus has to leave Criseyde on the morning after their consummation, we are told that he 'nevere yet swich hevy-nesse | Assayed hadde, out of so gret gladnesse...' (III. 1446–7). The idea that happiness itself incubates its opposite, and that humanity is caught up in a series of mutually enforcing oppositions, is stressed throughout *Troilus* and adumbrated in the *Book of the Duchess*. In the former poem the text does offer some form of 'solution' in the draconian exhortation at the end to leave the Wheel completely and turn 'holly [wholly]' to the enduring love of Christ (V. 1846), a proposition that the text in its desperation both enforces and subverts (see Chapter 3). The manner and the matter of this proposition owe a good deal to Boethius's *Consolation of Philosophy*, but the *Book of the Duchess* proceeds without the questionable aid of Boethius and gives us the man in black reliving his past happiness with Blanche in a manner that renews her death and his desolation at the end of the poem. Whatever consolation his dream of Blanche gives him has to be paid for in equal measure.

The *Book of the Duchess* is a study in a subject that fascinated Chaucer, and on which we shall have more to say – namely, uxoriousness. That the man in black's love for his 'swete wif' in its absoluteness – 'My suffisaunce, my lust, my lyf, | Myn hap, myn hele, and al my blesse, | My worldes welfare, and my

19

goddesse, I And I hooly hires and everydel' (ll. 1038–41) – was laying up trouble in store for him seems unmistakable. And yet, before we decide that a quasi-Boethian injunction to keep the world's goods in perspective *is* implied in the poem, we should note the sympathy of *Troilus and Criseyde* with the similarly immoderate recklessness of its own hero's love, sympathy indeed to the point of heroicization. When we first come across the man in black in the *Book* he is anomalously situated in a beautiful spring landscape, where the 'sorrows' of winter are all 'forgotten', 'For al the woode was waxen grene' (ll. 411–14), thus indicating by contrast the human inability for uncomplicated renewal, and the notion of human mourning and memorializing as both a privilege and a punishment. Humanity's problematic relation with the instinctual reflexes of the natural order is another favourite Chaucerian theme, as we shall see.

Chaucer, as everyone knows from passages in the 'Knight's Tale', the 'Prologue' to the *Legend of Good Women*, the opening of the 'General Prologue' itself, and elsewhere, is a celebrant of spring, renewal, the month of May, and so forth, but readers who prioritize this feature of the *Book of the Duchess* as consolatory obscure the sense of human alienation from it as described above. Again, the glory of the poet's role as *artifex* may be inferred from the poem, though future works like the *House of Fame* and *Parliament of Fowls* will problematize this too, as we shall see. Huppé and Robertson, in advancing a Christian reading of the *Book of the Duchess*, made much of the implied parallel with Dante's *Vita nuova* (*New Life*) in claiming that Blanche, like Beatrice, could lead her lover to the divine source of consolation after death. But the next major poem in Chaucer's chronology, the *House of Fame*, explicitly rejects Dantesque assurances, and quizzes the idea that the poet or his text has any access to authoritative truth. Some recent feminist writing on the *Book* would indeed see Blanche as defying any identification with Beatrice; thus Elaine Hansen develops some points in the Ellmann article above to show how the poem's quest is for the narrator to rescue the man in black from a love which feminizes and weakens him, and to reassert a stable masculine identity in the 'active' world by the end of the poem. Blanche's influence is thus to be destroyed, and the re-enactment of her death at the close tries to perform this, although the 'specter of Woman's and women's presence' continues to haunt male identity; as Hansen says, 'the problem is not only the woman outside but also what we might call the woman inside'.[4]

The *House of Fame* (usually accepted as written in the late 1370s or early 1380s, but certainly after Chaucer had made acquaintance with Italian literature) is a dream-vision that opens with an account of the various causes of dreams that have been put forward, and of its narrator's inability to decide between the competing theories, and his ignorance as to which class of dream his own belongs. This might seem the first challenge to Dantesque authoritativeness (the text has extensive references to Dante's *Divine Comedy*), in that, whereas dreams in the latter's work usually have the status of vision or prophecy, in this poem they are treated with a scepticism or at least agnosticism that, as critics like Sheila Delany have claimed, can be seen as typical of Chaucer's intellectual outlook generally (where the 'prophetic' dream is featured, as in the famous 'Nun's Priest's Tale', its recipient is a cock in a farmyard). The *House of Fame* thus begins with a virtual disclaimer about its 'correct' interpretation, an uncertainty endorsed by the fact that it was left unfinished; yet, in a further twist, the narrator then calls down curses on anyone who would 'mysdeme' (misinterpret) the dream described (l. 97), in what seems an outrageously provocative teasing of the reader's response. It is again typical of Chaucer that authorial or narratorial intention is often presented as uncertain or ambivalent, while, conversely, readerly interpretation (which he was clearly interested in) is frequently signalled as unavoidably subjective, a situation that has led one critic to explore the overlap between Chaucer's work and modern hermeneutics.[5]

The *House of Fame* problematizes the notion of 'meaning' then, not only what it is in this particular case but who is responsible for it, and the evident struggle of many critics to make sense of the poem suggests that the problematization has been successful. Of late, critics like Boitani have celebrated the poem as a post-modernist play of mixed narrative and discourse that revels precisely in its lack of an authoritative centre. In the first Book, the narrator dreams he is in a glass temple, decorated with scenes from the *Aeneid*. The narrator's interest is taken almost entirely with the Dido–Aeneas love-story from Book IV, which he recounts, with (as he admits) many of his own additions. At the

21

end of the first Book the dreamer leaves the temple, and is carried up into the aetherial regions by a comic and garrulous eagle (compare Dante's dream in *Purgatorio*, IX. 19–33, of being lifted by an eagle up to the 'sphere of fire'); the narrator's elevation is not, however, into the transcendental realms of divine reward and punishment but to the rather humbler location of the 'Hous of Fame' itself, where the eagle promises him he will hear some wonderful stories of love, to supplement his favourite reading matter. When he reaches the House, however, in the third and, presumably, final Book, he encounters not 'tidings' of love but the goddess Fame herself, seated on her throne and dispensing individuals' future reputations on earth in a totally arbitrary fashion. Thus people who have done good works come before her to be told that some will have a bad future fame, some a good, and some an indifferent one or none at all, while some villains will find themselves glorified on earth and so forth. Dismayed by this, the narrator leaves the House of Fame and comes across a labyrinthine construction of wickerwork, the House of Rumour, in which all sorts of tidings, rumours, and stories, compounds of truth and falsehood, endlessly circulate. The poem stops tantalizingly and famously on the narrator's sight of 'a man of gret auctorite' (l. 2158), who presumably might have offered narrator (and reader) some stable and reliable judgement in this hectic world of confusion, deceit, and false-dealing.

This dream which begins then with Dido and Aeneas and which seems to be concerned with 'love' gradually switches its focus to Fame, to the origins and bases of worldly reputation. This theme is indeed announced in the first Book, in Dido's lament over Aeneas's desertion of her and in the future reputation she fears for herself as a 'loose' woman, given that in loving Aeneas she has already broken her widow's vow of fidelity to her dead husband, Sichaeus, and, as the 'people' are already whispering, will be ready to give herself to the next man who comes along: ' "Loo, ryght as she hath don, now she I Wol doo eft-sones, hardely"– I Thus seyth the peple prively' (ll. 358–60). In her lament, Dido defends herself against any charge that she has proved an 'easy' conquest for Aeneas by invoking his oath of fidelity (or marriage), the 'bond' that 'ye have sworn with your ryght hond' (ll. 321–2), a claim already repudiated by Virgil himself in the *Aeneid*, who sees it as an act of self-deception on Dido's part: 'conjugium vocat; hoc praetexit nomine culpam' ('she calls it marriage; and with this term covers up her guilt', IV. 172). However, another account of the affair survives from antiquity, in Book VII of Ovid's *Heroides*, and this, like Book I of the *House of Fame*, seems far more sympathetic to Dido as the object of betrayal and condemnatory of Aeneas as betrayer. Indeed, the *House of Fame*, while claiming to be following Virgil's account, in fact splices this frequently with Ovid's, and with the narrator's own reconstruction.

What, then, the poem as a whole seems to be putting forward, is (or was) the 'truth'? Can we ever know it? Whence does it originate? Or is there no knowable truth, only stories, versions, rumours that all serve the interests of their tellers? Where did Virgil (or for that matter Ovid) get his 'information' from (the narrator claims to have got his in a dream, but what value have dreams?)? In the final Book of the poem, the tales that pass from mouth to mouth in the House of Rumour proceed to the House of Fame and are then broadcast on earth through Aeolus, the god of wind, as the source of that future reputation that Fame so randomly decrees. We are told that there are statues of poets and writers in Fame's house, whose works act as the most important and enduring channel for the dissemination of the raw material of rumour. Moreover, the eagle tells us in the second Book that every oral transmission on earth, be it speech, story, conversation, itself rises upwards to Fame's house (ll. 765–852), so that we have an endless circle of sound something like the rain-cycle, with oral stories passing into textual transmission that codifies reputation, in turn giving rise to more gossip that can be used as the basis of further stories, spoken or written and so on, *ad infinitum*. Were Virgil's doubts about Dido's conduct themselves founded on popular reputation? And did not the immense prestige of Virgil's text enshrine that reputation, and contribute powerfully to Dido's defamation?

These questions are given added point if we return to the poem's relationship with Dante, because in the famous second circle of *Inferno* described in canto V we find the lustful punished, those whose reason had been overwhelmed by sexual appetite, and among the figures from antiquity there we find none other than Dido. 'Fame' and the texts that codify it (for example, the *Aeneid*, much venerated by Dante) have here been used as the basis for Dido's condemnation, and there are several critics who see the strain of Dante-directed satire in Chaucer's poem as aimed, essentially, at the poet's claims of access to divine truth and at the submission to textual authority that supplements and reinforces those truth-claims. The *House of Fame* is the first of Chaucer's poems which take as their subject a woman hounded by a patrilineal succession of texts; we shall discuss this situation later with Criseyde and the Wife of Bath. Of course, the question arises that, if no one can know the 'truth' in Dido's case, then what justifies Chaucer's poem in seeming to take all the stories of male betrayal of females at face value, as Book I does (see ll. 388–426)? Several answers suggest themselves (not necessarily mutually exclusive), which will have to be refined when we look at Chaucer's later work. Perhaps the *House of Fame* can be seen as an immature phase of Chaucer's gender polemic, with the blanket condemnations of medieval anti-feminism here being simply contested by statements to the effect that all men are liars, deceivers, betrayers (see ll. 279–85; 301–10; 330-44), in a crude oppositionalism (compare my remarks on Chaucer as poet of deadlock above); perhaps the poem is ironizing, in a more sophisticated fashion, such oppositionalism; or perhaps Chaucer held it as axiomatic that, whatever the uncertainty of stories, rumours, versions, there is one truth that need not be qualified: that women get a raw deal.

The *House of Fame* is important in Chaucer's career because it anticipates so many of its author's later concerns: his interest in tales and tellers; his practice as a comic writer, employing a vigorously colloquial style (the eagle of Book II has been described as his first great comic character); his putative feminism (or at least anti-anti-feminism); and the creation of his own poetic persona. Alongside all the scepticism about the authoritativeness of authors, and of dreams, the picture of the narrator himself, 'Geffrey', in Book II (l. 729), as overweight, overworked, and befuddled, points to a debunking of the poet's role that again contrasts with Dante's self-assertions and that looks forward to the pilgrim-Chaucer of the *Tales*. The undoubted impact of Dante's work on Chaucer, in terms of his handling of dialogue and of a developing realism in his work, here finds itself taken up by a poem that in some ways deprecates the institution of poetry itself – in a typically English manner, some might be tempted to add.

3

Society, Sexuality, Spirituality

Many of the concerns we have traced in the dream-visions are explored more fully in *Troilus and Criseyde*, Chaucer's best-known and most substantial work outside the *Canterbury Tales*, and one completed in the mid-1380s. The concern with female reputation is at the heart of the work, and is voiced by Criseyde herself after her betrayal of Troilus in Book V, in terms similar to Dido's:

> Allas, of me, unto the worldes ende,
> Shal neyther ben ywriten nor ysonge
> No good word, for thise bokes wol me shende.
> O, rolled shal I ben on many a tonge!
>
> (v. 1058–61)

The interventions that the text makes to defend Criseyde from this defamation lie less in the narrator's overt sympathy for her in Book V – 'if I myghte excuse hire any wise, I For she so sory was for hire untrouthe, I Iwis, I wolde excuse hire yet for routhe' (ll. 1097–9) – than in the emphasis that pervades Chaucer's account of the affair on the powerlessness of Criseyde and the fierce manipulation she was subject to by the males around her. Indeed, she seems a classic case of a pawn in a patriarchal world. Within this world, to be sure, she gains what advantage she can through using her sexual attractiveness to win protection and partners, and it is a little difficult, after she has been dumped in the Greek camp through the sudden access of affection from her father, and with the bully-boy attentions of Diomede bearing down on her, to express moral outrage at the way she acquiesces in the face of this. In short, if we expect her to be a 'heroine', we will be disappointed, but Chaucer is testing his readers in this text by going beyond conventional literary expectations. As David Aers puts it, Chaucer 'has created a profound vision of a social individual whose bad faith was almost impossible to avoid, encouraged and prepared for by the habits and practices of the very society which would, of course, condemn such a betrayal with righteous moral indignation'.[1]

Troilus and Criseyde, then, can be read as Chaucer's deliberate intervention in 'the Criseyde tradition', a tradition that had come to him through various late-medieval texts recounting the fate of the Trojan lovers (classical texts concerned with the Troy legend have little to say about the pair, and their story seems first to be told in the *Roman de Troie* of Benoît de Sainte-Maure dating from the mid-twelfth century). Chaucer's immediate source was Boccaccio's *Filostrato* (*c.*1335), and this poem follows the tradition in seeing the story as one of female fickleness, endorsing Criseyde as a byword for self-seeking treachery ('thise bokes wol me shende', as Chaucer's Criseyde laments). Chaucer's text cannot change the 'facts', or details of the story, and indeed the poem announces right at the outset that eventually its subject will be how Criseyde 'forsook' Troilus (I. 56), but what it can do is to detail the circumstances that make any simple condemnation of this forsaking problematic.

Yet it is important, I think, that we do not regard Chaucer's poem as a simple 'whitewashing' of Criseyde, as some critics have tried to do. The poem – and this is typical of Chaucer – hardly lets us rest with any straightforward or unilateral verdict on the case. Even Aers, who in the reading referred to above is one of Criseyde's most passionate defenders, admits a kind of loophole in his talk of a bad faith that was '*almost* impossible to avoid' (emphasis added), though it is not clear how Aers himself understands the implications of that 'almost'. Book V dwells on Criseyde's isolation and vulnerability in the Greek camp, but it also dwells extremely powerfully on the bereft Troilus' agonizing wait for her return, and the reader is forced to empathize with both cases. That is why Criseyde's betrayal still 'hurts' exceedingly, and why, for example, her letter to Troilus at lines 1590–631, in which she attempts to keep her options open by promising a return to him, even though the decision has already been taken (by her or for her) to stay with Diomede, is not easy to justify. The final Book will talk about Criseyde's 'gilt' more than once (ll. 1096, 1775–6) at the same time as it conducts a forceful extenuation of that guilt; but the reader is not meant to think that any easy judgement is on offer.

This is one reason why Chaucer can address his poem as a 'tragedye' at line 1786; one element of the genre is often the ruin that overtakes confident moral categorization.

The problem then with some of the more unilateral feminist readings like Aers's is their reductiveness. Let me emphasize the pains Chaucer is taking to stress female oppression in the poem, culminating in the stanza in Book V where the narrator says he has spoken above all to warn women of men's betrayal: 'Beth war of men, and herkneth what I seye!' (l. 1785). But, whereas Dido's (and the narrator's) remarks in Book I of the *House of Fame* reach the kind of hysterical proposition that all women are good, all men bad, *Troilus and Criseyde* is working more subtly and more demandingly than this. Aers, somewhat like Dido, is only able to conduct his defence of Criseyde as exemplifying female subjugation by a wholesale attack on all the male protagonists in the poem and the social codes they embody, but a far more powerful case for Chaucer's critique of gender positions can be made if we understand Troilus too as no less a victim than Criseyde.

In short, there is no reason why a pro-Criseyde reading need be incompatible with a pro-Troilus reading, and I shall argue that the poem attempts to maintain this dual perspective. One problem with this latter reading is that, as everyone knows nowadays, Troilus is a complete wimp (at least in the eyes of many undergraduates). The text does indeed portray a kind of 'feminization' of Troilus that is sealed in Book V, where he is waiting powerlessly for his lover to come home from 'the front' in a startling gender-reversal, but all the way through the text we witness him as (generally) passive, tearful, coy, and frequently given to faints. The text is attempting to distance him from that world of ruthless pagan machismo into which he has been born; this unacceptable aspect of maleness is shovelled off onto Pandarus, who does most of the dirty work towards Criseyde of persuasion, deceit, and blackmail in the poem. But in arguing above that the text is not concerned to whitewash Criseyde, I have no wish now to claim this intention with regard to Troilus, and passages like II. 407–13, in which he offers to procure any of the women of his family for Pandarus in return for his services, would not permit this. Nevertheless, it does seem to me that the text is trying to cleanse Troilus in many ways of male brutalism, and, although the consummation scene in Book III talks of the sparrow-hawk catching the lark (ll. 1191–2), we must also remember that, when it comes to it, it is Pandarus (as the agent of male predatoriness) who has to throw the fainting Troilus into Criseyde's bed (ll. 1093–9). Troilus' subsequent pleasure in Criseyde is hardly bashful (ll. 1247–53) – indeed, the poem would find it difficult to celebrate sexuality if it was – but the poem clearly wants to distance it from brutality.

The male context in which Troilus figures is indeed a brutal one, right up to the highest level, given the frequent references to the rapes of the pagan gods that Chaucer introduces; the proem of Book III itself apostrophizes the power of Venus to induce the various 'incarnations' of Jupiter (as Europa's bull, Leda's swan, and so on) – 'in a thousand formes down hym sente | For love in erthe, and whom yow liste he hente' (ll. 20–1) – in a typical contrast the poem is (silently) making with Christianity, and the different mode of love governing its single Incarnation. Troilus prays to some of the pagan rapist gods before entering Criseyde's bedchamber later in the Book, and the whole action of the poem takes place, of course, against the backdrop of the Trojan War, which we are reminded several times was begun by Paris' abduction of Helen. But it is crucial, I think, to understand Troilus' story in the poem as one of his gradual disengagement from these cultural imperatives. This is most obviously enacted in Book IV, which includes a long interview between Pandarus and Troilus on how to respond to the arranged handover of Criseyde to the Greeks. Pandarus exhorts Troilus to 'act like a man' (see l. 538) and to resist the handover by detaining or abducting Criseyde:

> Why nylt thiselven helpen don redresse
> And with thy manhod letten al this grame?
> Go ravysshe here! Ne kanstow nat, for shame?
> And other lat here out of towne fare,
> Or hold here stille, and leve thi nyce fare.

(ll. 528–32)

Troilus' reply seals his dissociation from this pagan male ethic; not only does he bring up the lawless precedent of Paris' 'ravysshyng of wommen so by myght' (l. 548) but he expresses his determination (and repeats it later in the Book) of doing nothing without Criseyde's assent (ll. 637, 1526). In thus moving beyond a power-based concept of 'manhood', he represents in the final Book an abdication of power and a trusting fidelity that is finally rewarded with a quasi-Christian ascension to heaven in the poem's conclusion.

If we read the poem as showing the victimization of both its main protagonists, we should note that they are victimized by essentially different forces, and that this underlines the major structural dualism of the poem. When the God of Love's arrow hits Troilus 'atte fulle' near the beginning (I. 209), it signals the philosophical–religious discourse within which his problems will be explored throughout, whereas the troubles facing Criseyde will be bound up with social and secular pressures. Troilus is an idealist, whose love is constantly inscribed within a Boethian context of a search for the *summum bonum*, which is intuited but not understood through the 'lesser good' of Criseyde, who represents the 'shadow' of the true happiness unseen by the 'clouded' vision (on this see Book III of the *Consolation*). Troilus' fervent prayer to 'Benigne Love, thow holy bond of thynges' immediately after the consummation in Book III (l. 1261), and the 'Canticus Troili' near the end of that Book addressed to the same source (ll. 1744–71), point up the transcendence his love aspires to and that it finally achieves at the end of the poem. The sense of excess and idealism in his love for Criseyde indicates that she is not its 'proper' object; his victimization lies in the fact that within his pagan culture there is no one to point out the *summum bonum* to him, or how to reach it; likewise, none of the gods he prays to can represent it. All he has is Pandarus, who deliberately travesties Boethius' Lady Philosophy in teaching Troilus not how he can get 'off' Fortune's wheel completely, but only how he can learn to play it by cultivating an easy-come, easy-go 'philosophy' of life (impossible, of course, for someone with Troilus' powers of devotion).

With the switch to Book II and Criseyde's entering the poem, the agenda changes completely to focus on the social and sexual discriminations that she, as a woman, has to face. Her problems are immediate, practical, and everyday, and relate to how she can find and maintain freedom and space for herself in a world dominated by masculine authority. I have stressed above how seriously the text takes these concerns, and I do not wish to suggest that, in moving from Troilus' condition to hers, we are coming down from the 'heights' of spiritual dilemma into the realm of the mundane, in the pejorative sense of that term.

Indeed, it can be argued that the text shows Troilus' idealism as a luxury that only the privileged (e.g. royal males) can afford, whereas Criseyde's concerns are worldly because, as a woman, she has to look to things that Troilus need not concern himself with. But it would be a mistake to discount the Boethian discourse, and Troilus' association with it, as a merely conventional, 'medieval' element within the text – in other words, as one that Chaucer himself had no real interest in, or only in so far as he wanted to show it as a 'mystification' of contemporary social practices.

David Aers's Criseyde-centred reading, which represents one end of the spectrum of response, does this. The poem's interests are regarded as primarily feminist-sociological, with the lovers' marvellous and heart-warming intimacy in Book III being killed off by a hostile patriarchal culture in which Troilus himself is damningly implicated (see above). Aers reads the poem as a kind of proto-D. H. Lawrence novel, with the love of the bedchamber (cf. the gamekeeper's cottage) being martyred to a hostile social reality. At the other extreme is the Robertsonian reading of Chauncey Wood (1984), for whom the spiritual quest of the poem, and Troilus' stumbling journey towards the metaphysical illumination he experiences at the end, are primary, the love between the protagonists being discounted as mere bodily lust, a thing of this world that Troilus gets reprehensibly mired in.[2] Just as Aers was not interested in Boethius, so Wood rejects any serious Chaucerian intervention in social or sexual politics, other than the claim that Chaucer is sternly moralizing against the royal household being corrupted by its libido, in the wake of Edward III's affair with Alice Perrers.

That the poem has lent itself to these entirely antithetical readings reaffirms its powerful duality, a duality that should not be brushed aside so readily. Several readings, not only Wood's, demonize sexuality as presented in the poem,[3] whereas others, like Aers's, glorify it. In my opinion, the poem wishes to realize fully the potential for beauty and ecstasy of a love that incorporates sexual pleasure, at the same time as it promotes a mindfulness of the dangers and disappointments liable to overtake that love, in comparison with a Christ who is 'best to love' and unchangingly faithful, and overtly introduced into the poem as its *summum bonum* at the conclusion (v. 1842–8). The opposing 'pull' of such loves is at the heart of the poem, and readings that easily discount one or the other are ducking out of the dilemma the poem asks its readers to experience. The cost of the lovers' happiness in Book III, particularly in Troilus' case, incapable as he is of circumspection, is seen fully in the succeeding Books, where memory of the heights he has scaled only intensifies his woe in being abandoned (a position which I noted above had been adumbrated in the *Book of the Duchess*). From this it is all too easy to argue that the poem does have a straightforward Boethian agenda, arguing for holding this world's pleasures at arm's length, or even forsaking them completely. But a moment's reflection shows that this cannot be the case. Boethius wrote the *Consolation of Philosophy* when he was in prison, having lost everything, as he tells us in the work itself: power, status, wealth. From such a position of calamity it makes entirely good sense to argue for the defectiveness of this world's 'goods', to rejoice in having lost them, and to claim such calamity as a blessing. In this sense, the *Consolation* is probably the most spectacular example of 'positive thinking' ever produced. But the context is entirely different when the protagonist is young, and this world's joy still lies in the future, and waiting to be experienced, not in the past; indeed, when she is waiting in bed in the next room. To adopt a Boethian distance here may be what the *Troilus* is recommending (as it clearly does in its conclusion), but at the same time it shows the impracticability of such a recommendation. Rather than being an endorsement of Boethian- ism (or *as well* as being this), the poem can be read as a critique of it, along the lines that many readers of Boethius have felt themselves: that what the *Consolation* has to say is marvellous in theory, but pretty unworkable in practice. No position in *Troilus and Criseyde* (Boethius included) escapes interrogation.

I am suggesting, then, that the poem represents a sustained desire to affirm opposing things, not in the sense of that comfortable or 'positive' oppositionalism referred to by Peter Elbow,[4] but in an extremely uncomfortable manner. This seems to me distinctively Chaucerian. The poem's 'target audience' is precisely the 'yonge, fresshe folkes, he or she' (v. 1835), those most likely to experience the imperatives of sexuality; as I remarked above, the poem both enforces and subverts its desperate attempt to 'handle' sexuality in the concluding exhortation to this audience to turn 'wholly' to Christ. What is certainly not on offer at the end of the poem, in spite of the claims of some critics (such as Ida L. Gordon) to see a positive mediation there, is any integration of Christianity and sexuality, and this sense of a world riven apart by conflicting imperatives is an issue sustained by Chaucer throughout the *Canterbury Tales*, as we shall see. Because the *Troilus* is set in a pagan world, the protagonists (and the text) have greater freedom to celebrate the delights of sexuality in order to bring out the full force of the oppositions within the poem, but in the *Tales*, a new and complicating factor is brought into play – namely, the presence of the medieval Church and its official veto on sexual pleasure.

4

Readers, Listeners, Audience

There is still much speculation and uncertainty about the identity
of Chaucer's audience, and about the venue in which his works
were 'performed'. In *Troilus and Criseyde*, the narrator frequently
addresses an audience envisaged as listening to the work in oral
delivery:

> And forthi if it happe in any wyse,
> That here be any lovere in this place
> That herkneth, as the storie wol devise,
> How Troilus com to his lady grace...

(II. 29–32)

In the famous frontispiece to a manuscript of the poem in Corpus
Christi, Cambridge (MS 61), a figure is shown reciting the poem to
an assembly from a lectern, but whether this represents actual
practice, or is precisely an illustration of the narrator–audience
relationship presented within the text, is uncertain. Certainly the
Troilus, which of all Chaucer's poems has the most exhortations
(even if not consistent ones) to an audience, has a particular
reason for staging the semblance of a direct, oral delivery. If and
where it was so delivered, however (for example, within the royal
court), remain uncertain.[1] The *House of Fame*'s narrator also
frequently represents himself as speaking directly to a listening
audience; yet this poem, which also posits a narrator who is
'bookish' and fond of private reading (ll. 654–60), and which, as
we saw above, is immersed in a literary tradition that includes
Virgil, Ovid, and Dante, points up nicely the historical position of
Chaucer's work at an orality–literacy confluence. There seems
little doubt that Chaucer's poems would have been read aloud,
perhaps by the author himself; but there are many references in
his work (as in all the dream-visions) to reading, as opposed to
listening – notably in the injunction in the 'Miller's Prologue' to

33

those who wish to avoid bawdiness: 'Turne over the leef and chese another tale' (l. 3177). It is interesting to note, however, that the previous line addresses these readers as those who may not like to 'hear' such a tale.

Whatever our uncertainty about the contemporary modes of reception of his work, there is no doubt that Chaucer was keenly attentive to the concept of audience, and the *Canterbury Tales* is an assembly not only of tellers but of listeners too, and the work pays full attention to their ways of listening. But before turning to these, we need to think a little more about the reception of *Troilus and Criseyde*, because some evidence is given as to what this was in (presumably) Chaucer's next poem, the *Legend of Good Women*. In the 'Prologue' to this poem the narrator imagines himself (in a dream) being upbraided by the God of Love for having dared to write the *Troilus* (and some other works), on the grounds that Love is given a bad name through the poem's presentation of the fickleness of lovers – female lovers, that is:

> Hast thow nat mad in Englysh ek the bok
> How that Crisseyde Troylus forsok,
> In shewynge how that wemen han don mis?
>
> (G version, ll. 264–6)

After our discussion of *Troilus* above, this will strike us as a pretty unfair accusation, in that the poem does well nigh all it can to avoid the simple imputation of Criseyde's 'wikednesse' which the God of Love now lays at Chaucer's door; as I have said, he can rather be seen as intervening in the 'Criseyde tradition' in the attempt to rescue her from the charge. The God of Love's reading of the poem, however, is unqualified and unsophisticated: Chaucer should not have told the story of a 'bad' woman when there were so many good women to choose from, and as reparation Chaucer is now set the task of writing a catalogue of such good women, who remained faithful to their loves even at the cost of death. Typically, the bumbling Chaucer–narrator figure makes no attempt to defend himself from these charges, or to expound on his aims in writing *Troilus*; in Lisa Kiser's study of the *Legend* he is rather seen as jokingly submitting to 'an audience's demanding stupidity'[2] in preferring simple-minded exempla of either 'good' or 'bad' women to anything more strenuous, and proceeds to fulfil Cupid's request.

There may be an element of humour about the accusations presented in the 'Prologue' to the *Legend*, but they do reflect a serious underlying situation. At the end of *Troilus* itself, the poet is already apologizing for having selected Criseyde's 'gilt' as his subject, and promises there to write next about faithful women (v. 1772–8), as if he himself is aghast at his own temerity in writing the work. I think there is a genuine nervousness here about what he has done in *Troilus and Criseyde* in departing from the simple gender polarity we found in *The House of Fame*, and a recognition that putting moral cases within a full context of motivation, conditioning, and ideology may go too far beyond his immediate audience's cultural horizons. Modern readers have often claimed *Troilus* as the ancestor of the realist novel, but Chaucer himself seems to have had worries about being George Eliot. What is interesting is that he never attempted anything like *Troilus and Criseyde* again, and in the *Tales*, as we shall see, he questions simple exempla not so much by trying to go beyond them in his own work but by satirizing his audience's taste for them.

The command to Chaucer in the F version of the *Legend*'s 'Prologue' (ll. 496–7), to give the poem to the queen (Anne, wife of Richard II) once it is completed, has sometimes been taken to hint at a royal displeasure with Chaucer's work for which the *Legend* is reparation. Chaucer, however, never finished the poem, breaking off in the middle of the ninth legend, the story of Hypermnestra, and, however fascinating the poem is in Chaucer's development, it has never found popularity with readers (the 'Prologue' aside); the common reaction seems to be that the legends are repetitive and diffuse, with the author himself constantly making flippant or inconsequential asides that seem to indicate his own frustration with the exemplum form or inability to concentrate on it.

In the *Canterbury Tales* Chaucer continues to be very attentive to the limited interpretative habits that might characterize some of his audience, notably in the 'marriage-group' section (running from the 'Wife of Bath's Prologue' to the 'Franklin's Tale'), so named by Kittredge in a seminal article of 1911–12.[3] The 'Clerk's Tale', recounting the total humility and obedience of 'poor Griselda' in the face of the brutal orders of her husband, is received by the pilgrims on various levels. The Clerk himself, after telling the tale, suggests that it should be understood as a moralization about accepting patiently the trials God sends us, which are given to prove and strengthen our metal, and not as a recommendation to actual wives to put up with their husbands' tyranny to the extent that Griselda did (ll. 1142–62). He cannot, however, help adding 'one word' that does contrast Griselda as a wifely model with the degenerate state of modern wives, represented as the 'sect' of the Wife of Bath (ll. 1163–76). The Merchant, who tells the following tale, has no interest in the religious dimension of the 'Clerk's Tale', and in his 'Prologue' understands Griselda as a simple paragon he can use to lambast his own wife's shortcomings (ll. 1223–5). He then proceeds to tell a tale that will illustrate such shortcomings in wives, again eagerly seized on at its conclusion by the Host, eager to find confirmation of the 'sleightes and subtilitees' of women (l. 2421), in which his own wife too is so depressingly well versed.

The 'Merchant's Tale', however, is an extremely sophisticated and multi-levelled narrative (we shall return to it below), and there is a delicious irony in Chaucer's putting it in the mouth of a teller who is seeking a simple expression of anti-feminism. Although May might easily be seen as a 'bad' woman (cold, faithless, opportunist), the Tale clearly presents her qualities as a consequence of the patriarchal tyrannies she is subject to; behind every bad woman lurks a bad man. This is a reading which neither the teller, the Merchant, nor the commentator, the Host, seems to have any inkling of, in their reductive motivations, even though a consistent chain of association in the text endorses it. For example, Pluto is introduced into the tale shaking his head over the treasonable behaviour of women, a speech introduced by the reminder that he originally abducted, or 'ravysshed', his wife Proserpine, in a clear parallel with January's simple decision to 'have' May for wife (ll. 2225 ff). Men are cast as the originators of the trouble they bring on their own heads, and, when the Merchant in his 'Prologue' suggests his wife would be more than a match for the devil (ll. 1219–20), he unwittingly associates himself with the Pluto of his tale (king of the underworld) and through him with January. The tale therefore casts men not only as 'devils', but, in their inability to reflect on their own incrimination in the wifely conduct they are castigating, stupid devils at that.

Although the 'marriage group' is the section of the *Tales* where men–women relations are debated most vigorously, such a subject is never far away from the *Tales* as a whole. Kittredge, in arguing that the group concluded with the 'Franklin's Tale', was, like many erstwhile critics, on the look-out for a benign Chaucer who would air divisions and then find a pleasing 'solution' for them. In seeing the tales as primarily expressions (or 'soliloquies') of their tellers' outlooks and personalities (though not as subversions of such outlooks, as we argued with the 'Merchant's Tale' above), Kittredge found in the affable, gentlemanly Franklin the perfect voice for that picture of happy mutuality between husband and wife with which his tale opens: 'freendes everych oother moot obeye, | If they wol longe holden compaignye' (ll. 762–3). This, then, is Chaucer's own solution: not wives who are simply dominant or doormats, nor husbands who are masters or cuckolds, but partners who both rule and are ruled by each other.

This suspiciously anodyne-sounding resolution is, however, undermined by the 'Franklin's Tale' itself, where, under the stress of the wife's promise to commit adultery, the husband takes absolute charge and, ruled by an inflexible code of honour, commands his wife to keep her promise 'up peyne of deeth' and at great emotional cost to himself (ll. 1479–86). But, even if one had no suspicions about marital equality not surviving intact during the course of the tale, it is clear that the 'Franklin's Tale' hardly addresses the problems thrown up solely by the first piece in the 'marriage group', the 'Wife of Bath's Prologue'. This introduces us to the marriage market in fourteenth-century England, the economic arrangements that govern it, the Church's overseeing of it, and the prevailing anti-feminism that bears down on it; the 'Franklin's Tale', as a Breton lay with a romantic, magical and pre-mercantile setting, can hardly provide an 'answer' to the socio-economic problems of medieval marriage, even if one can accept the resolution proclaimed within it. It is, in fact, a fantasy romance, and the Wife of Bath herself had already tried to escape into this world of happiness ever after in the tale she told, following on from her 'Prologue'. But she is unable to stay in this world (as we shall see), and returns to 'reality' with a bump. The notion of the 'marriage group' is still used in Chaucer criticism to describe the above sequence of tales, but no one would now claim, I think, that the issues there were resolved, nor that the relationship between the tellers is paramount. These tales comprise many different genres, and raise questions that go far beyond the immediate occasion of a marriage 'debate' between the speakers.

As an example, in the 'Franklin's Tale' Chaucer continues to satirize the exemplum tradition. While Dorigen is agonizing over her promise to commit adultery with Aurelius, she voices a lament of just over 100 lines in which she lists all the noble wives and maidens of antiquity who killed themselves rather than besmirch their good name. At the end, the narrator notes casually: 'Thus pleyned Dorigen a day or tweye, | Purposynge evere that she wolde deye' (ll. 1457–8), a statement that undercuts any serious possibility that these 'good women' could be models of action for Dorigen, or that exemplarity is any sort of example in her situation. The Wife of Bath herself voices the fact of how women are persecuted not only by aggressive anti-feminist images, but by male examples of 'positive' womanhood:

> trusteth wel, it is an impossible
> That any clerk wol speke good of wyves,
> But if it be of hooly seintes lyves,
> Ne of noon oother womman never the mo.

(ll. 688–91)

In the 'Franklin's Tale', we have a distance between Dorigen and her 'models'; in the 'Clerk's Tale', Griselda is still a paragon, but, compared with the stories of the 'good women' of the *Legend*, the psychological relationship between her and her husband is rather more delicate and complex; and, although May might be seen as 'bad' in the 'Merchant's Tale', her flaws are socially constructed rather than inherent to her as an individual. Indeed, it is difficult to talk of any of these personae as 'individuals' at all; Chaucer may be questioning simple models of exemplarity, but he is not doing it, as he did in *Troilus and Criseyde*, through a detailed and far-reaching attention to the case of a single protagonist contending with cultural institutions. The *Tales* are much shorter, of course, and there is no space for such development. Elsewhere in the *Tales*, Chaucer himself is happy to deal in 'hooly seintes lyves', as in the 'Man of Law's Tale' and the 'Second Nun's Tale'. The first of these recounts the legend of Custance (or Constancy) through a series of dramatic persecutions that only strengthen her Christian faith; tales like these may be less to the taste of many modern readers, but Chaucer was interested in all types of discourse, and in the interplay and tensions between them, and in the *Canterbury Tales* puts a series of competing and antagonistic world-views, often linked (though not necessarily in a simple way) to the particular outlook and social position of the tellers. Thus, to return to the Man of Law, it makes every kind of sense to have a tale promoting a rather hard-line Christian orthodoxy in the mouth of such a teller; the very name, 'Man of Law', prepares us for the anti-feminism and conservatism that will follow in his tale. Thus, within the proliferating dialogue of the *Tales* we have to be very careful about attributing any of the 'views' voiced there to Chaucer himself, though my argument thus far that Chaucer was resistant to (or at least sceptical towards) the prevailing anti-feminism of his culture is supported by the extent of his engagement with this issue throughout his works.

5

Nature, Culture, Carnival

Before resuming our discussion of the *Tales*, it will be helpful to look at a final dream-vision that anticipates several aspects of that discussion. The *Parliament of Fowls* is generally dated to the first half of the 1380s, and, though one of Chaucer's shortest major poems, is also one of his most intriguing. The narrator in his dream enters the garden of Love (as in the *Romance of the Rose*), where he visits the temple of Venus with its attendants like Pleasure, Beauty, Youth, but also Foolhardiness, Flattery, Desire, and sees Venus herself in provocative display in its innermost sanctum: 'Hyre gilt heres with a golden thred I Ibounden were, untressed as she lay, I And naked from the brest unto the hed...' (ll. 267–9). Leaving the temple, he then comes across the 'noble goddesse Nature' standing on a hill of flowers (ll. 302–3); it is St Valentine's Day, and she is here to supervise the annual pairing-off of the birds, in all their different species. On her wrist she holds her pride and joy, a beautifully formed female eagle, and contention arises when three different male eagles sue for her hand (or claw). While the lower orders of birds become impatient with the business, wanting to mate with rather less ceremony, a debate is staged over which of the eagles has the best claim, and how to resolve the deadlock; in the end the female eagle herself is given the choice of mate, and asks for a year's delay in making it. Nature grants this, the rest of the birds pair off, and some sing a roundel in Nature's honour celebrating the birth of the year and the death of winter. At this point the dreamer awakes, the whole poem with its dense set of cultural and literary references occupying a mere 699 lines.

One way in which this poem anticipates the *Tales* is in its humorous contrast of discourses between the aristocratic address of the eagle wooers (though the second eagle is noticeably blunter

40

than the first, ll. 450–62) and the more demotic 'lower' birds: 'Whan shal youre cursede pletynge have an ende?' they ask the eagles (l. 495). Whether the hierarchy of birds is seen as representing different classes in human society, or as the natural order itself, with the eagles' courting at the top standing for human societal conventions as opposed to the simple instinctual drive of the lower creatures, makes little difference. Human beings (or the more 'civilized' portion of them) do not normally go round expressing their sexuality simply by jumping on each other, but their courtship is subject to elaborate codes, linguistic, legalistic, aesthetic; in short, love (at least in its 'courtly' guise) is a 'craft so long to lerne', as the very first line of the poem says. What the *Parliament* focuses on is the difficult place that humanity thus occupies within the realm of Nature, and how that which sets us apart from the rest of that order is both privilege and penalty, a theme that echoes the *Book of the Duchess* (see Chapter 2). The fact that the female eagle is given a choice, that the contract to delay is accepted, and that the dispute is in the form of a debate, all this points to the importance and prestige of human conventions; but the result, of course, is that the instincts are not satisfied and that the joyous roundel the birds sing at the end, which in its circular form emphasizes the seasonal cycle and the ordering powers of the goddess Nature, leaves humanity somewhere on the outside. And, of course, there is one final stanza after the roundel is completed in which the dreamer wakes up and suggests that he is still without the 'answer' he is looking for, as if in graphic illustration of that exclusion.

The temple of Venus is itself a spectacular example of the human codification of the instincts, discussed above. With its allegorical figures it is a shrine to sexuality that takes on an elaborately artificial form; the very situation of a temple being situated in Nature's garden indicates that for human beings it is 'natural' to be artificial, or again that the instincts have to be mediated through ritual, ceremony, and convention. On the walls of the temple are paintings illustrating the disastrous fate of many figures from classical legend (ll. 284–94), those whose love led them to break laws and conventions through adultery, incest, or indiscriminate lustfulness, leading to death or madness. If the obstacles to any simple expression of sexuality akin to the rest of creation are here referred to, it is important to note that precisely such difficulties are seen as giving rise to story, legend, and, in the form of the temple, 'art' itself (and by extension the poem Chaucer is writing); the aesthetic construct is seen as a deferral and reinscription of the sexual drive. This sublimation is again entirely 'natural' to human beings, but it does mean that our place in the natural order is a complex and ambiguous one.

Frequently in the *Canterbury Tales* we find ourselves in the arena of human sexuality, and just as frequently we find a repeat of the encounter between these forces and societal and religious governance; in the Wife of Bath's famous protest, 'Allas, allas! That evere love was synne!' (l. 614). In the *Parliament*, one of the paintings in the temple is of Troilus (l. 291), and, as we have seen, Chaucer soon afterwards took this story to produce his longest study of the 'confrontation' between sexual and spiritual imperatives, and also his longest study of human sexuality *per se*, showing that this is not incompatible with altruism and fidelity (i.e. not a synonym for mere 'lust'). But within the smaller space of the individual Tales, Chaucer narrows his concentration once again to consider sexuality less philosophically, one might say, and more in its social context. We are no longer in the world of classical legend, but in that of the contemporary fabliau, where sexuality and bawdiness are often indistinguishable.

The first instance of this in the *Tales* is in the 'Miller's Tale'. In his 'Prologue' the Miller says he is telling this to 'quite' the 'Knight's Tale', which opens the Canterbury sequence (l. 3127); that is, whatever the Knight has done, he can provide a retort to it that will be fully equal. It is clear that Chaucer has planned the opening two Tales as a kind of oppositional balance (one is tempted to say 'deadlock' again). The 'Knight's Tale' is a story of human stoicism under divine persecution, with the marriage between Palamon and Emily at the end representing the human will to endure in the face of the random cruelties of life, like Arcite's sudden death in his hour of triumph; as Theseus recommends, we must 'maken vertu of necessitee, I And take it weel that we may nat eschue' (ll. 3042–3). Following this serious and sombre opening, we have the drunken Miller in holiday mood coming forward with his tale of revelry and pleasure, and actually repeating Arcite's phrase on the solitude of the 'cold grave', 'Allone, withouten any compaignye' (ll. 2778–9), to describe Nicholas's perfumed and book-filled bedchamber, where he secretly hatches his plots to seduce Alison (l. 3204). The 'getting even' that the 'Miller's Tale' represents lies not so much in the Miller's reproducing the 'courtly-love' triangle of the 'Knight's Tale' in comic and bawdy mode, as in the completely differing world-views, laughter versus seriousness we might say, that these two Tales embody.

In fact, as several scholars have pointed out, these first two Tales offer an exemplary illustration of Mikhail Bakhtin's theories of the carnivalesque, particularly in his study of Rabelais, *Rabelais and his World*, first translated into English in 1968. Bakhtin holds that 'the men of the Middle Ages participated in two lives: the official and the carnival life. Two aspects of the world, the serious and the laughing aspect, coexisted in their consciousness'.[1] This latter world, the 'carnival life', Bakhtin sees in a constant opposition to the world of 'gloomy seriousness' that is promulgated through the official teachings of the medieval Church: carnival and its laughter 'offered a completely different, nonofficial, extraecclesiastical and extrapolitical aspect of the world, of man, and of human relations; they built a second world in which all medieval people participated more or less, in which they lived during a given time of the year.'[2] Carnival images and activities often took the form of parodies of sacred and serious teaching, or of a grotesque inversion of it, such as the various parodic liturgies that Bakhtin lists (the Liturgy of the Drunkards, Liturgy of the Gamblers), or the 'Feast of Fools' in its various guises, the crowning of boy- or animal-bishops, the so-called Easter or Christmas laughter.[3] The 'Wife of Bath's Prologue', for example, has long been associated with one of these parodic forms, the *sermon joyeau* or comic sermon. And it is important to note, as Bakhtin says, that often the most active producers and consumers of these folk forms were clerics themselves: 'we know that men who composed the most unbridled parodies of sacred texts and of cults often sincerely accepted and served religion',[4] thus returning us to the 'coexistence' of these two worlds within the individual.

The 'Miller's Tale' is Chaucer's most emphatic and uncomplicated exercise in the carnivalesque. A bawdy retelling of sacred story, in that an old carpenter with a young wife is 'visited' not by the Holy Spirit but by the exuberant Nicholas, who sings 'Angelus ad virginem' with his own carnivalizing intent (l. 3216), it is a tale rife with carnivalesque images and with the laughter they give rise to. It is a tale of play, of licence, of holiday, with its scenes of pleasure and of farce constantly set off against the 'other' world of ecclesiastical routine and order:

> And thus lith Alison and Nicholas,
> In bisynesse of myrthe and of solas,
> Til that the belle of laudes gan to rynge,
> And freres in the chauncel gonne synge.

(ll. 3653-6)

Nicholas, as the main instigator of this mirth, is a student, and thus occupies a privileged place of freedom in society (an attenuated form of carnival might still be seen as existing in 'Rag Week') that contrasts in the Tale with the role of John, the hard-working, pious, elderly husband who constantly congratulates himself on this identity ('Thynk on God, as we doon, men that swynke [work]', he exhorts Nicholas, l. 3491), and who, as the representative of 'gloomy seriousness', gets his come-uppance in the Tale. His fate as an object of mockery at the end, with everyone turning 'al his harm unto a jape' (l. 3842), is in keeping with the carnivalesque punishment of 'individual incarnations of... prevailing thought, law, and virtues', in Bakhtin's phrase.[5] It is important to note the dominance of laughter at the end of the Tale, reproduced in three audiences: the audience internal to the Tale (John's neighbours), the pilgrim-listeners, and in us the readers. And among Chaucer's pilgrims no one is excluded from that laughter (save the Reeve, of course, who has a personal grudge against the Tale); Bakhtin claims that all medieval people participated in carnival, and that 'the medieval culture of folk humour actually belonged to all the people. The truth of laughter embraced and carried away everyone; nobody could resist it.'[6] At the end of the 'Miller's Tale' laughter cuts across social boundaries to bring the pilgrims together as a 'folk' community; we are not told that even those saintly brothers the Parson and Plowman grieve at it.

The other important carnivalesque aspect of the Tale centres on the role of the young wife, Alison. The recurring carnival images of eating, drinking, procreating, defecation, and everything associated with the 'bodily lower stratum' are seen by Bakhtin as celebrating the permanent renewal of the material world, as opposed to the transcendental urges of religion that would negate this world. Bakhtin reads the genre of the fabliau (though he does

44

not seem to have known Chaucer's work specifically) and its favourite theme of the cuckolding of an old husband by a young wife, as a symbolic 'uncrowning' of the old order by the new, particularly in a seasonal sense: 'in this system of images the cuckolded husband assumes the role of uncrowned old age, of the old year, and the receding winter. He is stripped of his robes, mocked, and beaten'.[7] The most celebrated carnivalesque gesture in the Tale, and one of the commonest generally, the 'misplaced kiss', is, in its replacement of the face by the buttocks, a symbolic enactment of that 'overturning', top becoming bottom, which is the essence of carnival's opposition to hierarchy and authority. In the person of Absolon, the authority assaulted could be the Church, given that Absolon is a cleric, aristocratic refinement, given that he is a would-be 'courtly' lover, or more generally the authority of gender, since the misplaced kiss has a knock-on effect which leads to all three men in the Tale being 'uncrowned' at the end and Alison escaping unharmed. Certainly the sense of the energies of youthful renewal overcoming the old year is emphasized by the next Tale in the Canterbury sequence, that of the Reeve, where the narrator's 'Prologue' begins with a long description of the sourness and aridity of old age. The 'Reeve's Tale' that follows attempts to pay the Miller back for mocking elderly carpenters (the Reeve's own profession) by telling a tale about a disreputable miller who gets cuckolded in turn. But many readers have commented on the bitterness of the 'Reeve's Tale': at first sight a fabliau not dissimilar to the Miller's, it has an uncouthness of characterization and a grimy portrayal of human sexuality that point up by contrast the boisterous humour of the 'Miller's Tale' and its fresh carnivalesque spirit.

The concept of carnival might seem one sort of answer to the problem explored in the *Parliament of Fowls*, in that, in tales like the Miller's, human sexuality is expressed as an uncomplicated, joyous, and animalistic part of the natural order (expressed particularly in the animal images that invest the portrait of Alison, ll. 3233–70), rather than as alienated from it by cultural codes and prohibitions. But the 'Miller's Tale' is just one Tale; and, if there Chaucer is expressing the carnivalesque outlook, this is not to say that it has any final validity. In other Tales, like the Knight's, we see the reverse picture, of a world not viewed in holiday mood but largely as a Boethian 'thurghfare [thoroughfare] ful of wo' in Egeus'

45

phrase (l. 2847) that we must travel as best we can. Yet other Tales, like the Merchant's, can be viewed as direct anti-carnivalesque satire; and the 'Wife of Bath's Prologue' and her Tale complicate the carnival theme still further, and call into question, perhaps, Bakhtin's rather simple polarity between the two medieval worlds, the laughing and the serious, that co-habit in the individual consciousness (on this, see the following chapter).

At first sight, the 'Merchant's Tale' does seem another exercise on the carnivalesque theme, with old age and the 'receding winter' being mocked and 'stripped of his robes' in the person of January, cuckolded by his wife, the 'fresshe' May. Yet few would claim this as a celebratory or 'laughing' tale of uncrowning, as in the 'Miller's Tale'. January's calculating self-gratification has nothing of the innocent obtuseness of John; the description of the wedding night and of January's senile lust, with May being brought to bed 'as stille as stoon' (l. 1818), is disgusting in the extreme, and the carefully maintained impassiveness of May throughout intensifies the atmosphere of emotional aridity. The 'uncrowning' of the old husband itself, performed by May and Damyan in the pear tree, is no joyous assault on the old order but rather the consummation of the Tale's bitter mood; sexuality here is no source of pleasure (for either partner) but something nasty, brutish, and short:

> Ladyes, I prey yow that ye be nat wrooth;
> I kan nat glose, I am a rude man –
> And sodeynly anon this Damyan
> Gan pullen up the smok, and in he throng.

> (ll. 2350–3)

By the end of the Tale, May is pregnant (whether by January or Damyan is a nice point), but, in spite of the emphasis on procreation and on seasonal renewal – this latter underlined by the unexpected presence of Proserpine and Pluto in the Tale, with Proserpine being above ground in a mythological endorsement of the return of Spring – the Tale feels anything but 'Spring-like', and the difference with, say, the end of the *Parliament of Fowls* and the birds' roundel welcoming the return of the sun is marked. Although, as noted in Chapter 2, Chaucer's popular reputation is based in part on his verses in praise of Spring and in particular of 'the month of May', the repeated adjective 'fresshe' for the character May in the 'Merchant's Tale' only emphasizes the sardonic and anti-laudatory tone of the whole piece. The Tale's assault on any affirmatory response to the natural order and its season of rebirth is a matter not simply of tone but of context; the seduction (if that is not too indirect a term) of May in the tree clearly restages the fall of Eve, with Damyan playing the role of the serpent tempter, and the whole setting of January's pleasure garden not only mirrors the garden of Eden but deliberately gestures, by antithesis, to the walled garden that commonly imaged the Virgin Mary. In other words, there is an important religious dimension to the Tale which would site the protagonists, and human sexuality more generally, within a 'fallen' context, and the references to original sin substantiate the disgust and displeasure at human coupling amply displayed there.

The 'Merchant's Tale' indeed, and more particularly its central setting of the garden, is like an arena in which, once more for Chaucer, two worlds collide, that of Christian orthodoxy and that of pagan natural energies, and there is little doubt that it is emphasis on the former which determines the flavour of the Tale. Here then any carnivalesque 'subversion' is itself subverted, and it is of a piece with this that the Tale ends, not with the old husband broken and uncrowned, as with the 'Miller's Tale', but with his authority renewed, and May being escorted back home: 'to his palays hoom he hath hire lad' (l. 2415). Winter will come back, Pluto will lead Proserpine back under the ground; there is no permanent defeat of the order of 'gloomy seriousness', in Bakhtin's phrase, nor of (to return to the concerns of the previous chapter) male power, but only temporary holidays from them. And it will be obvious, I think, that the Merchant's is a brilliant example of a Tale that cannot be explained simply at the level of the teller; although we saw above how the tale contravenes the Merchant's own anti-feminism, its many levels go much beyond this to consider anew issues that had obsessed Chaucer throughout his writing.

In suggesting the 'Merchant's Tale' as an anti-carnivalesque piece, I again do not want to propose this as demonstrative of Chaucer's own thinking, though clearly an uncomplicated materiality/sexuality celebrating this world's renewal and humanity's place within this is something he had problems with, as his other works show. The 'Merchant's Tale', like the

Miller's, is a particular viewpoint, a particular discourse, and the *Canterbury Tales* is an anthology of various discourses. In any case, Bakhtin would agree that, in the conjunction of two Tales like this, or more graphically of the first and second Tales, the Knight's and Miller's, Chaucer is demonstrating a typical medieval dualism. The real triumph of the carnivalesque, and its overthrow of fear, gloom, and the wintry old year, will have to wait till Rabelais's *Gargantua and Pantagruel*, with its sustained emphasis on feasting and festivity, its celebration of the belly and the womb, its prolonged utopian banquet 'for all the world'. The people of the Middle Ages, according to Bakhtin, were not at this stage; whatever the literature of laughter, 'the consciousness of each individual could not free itself from fear and weakness. Freedom granted by laughter often enough was mere festive luxury.'[8] And the permanent 'co-existence' of fear and laughter, gloom and festivity, 'the official and the carnival life', in medieval consciousness is illustrated by Bakhtin through the case of the contemporary manuscript and ecclesiastical building, where adjacent to the most pious images we find the most comical and grotesque, the saint and the gargoyle: 'however, in medieval art a strict dividing line is drawn between the pious and the grotesque; they exist side by side but never merge.'[9] In this reading then, especially with the careful antithesis and demarcation between the first two Tales, Chaucer would come across as a typical man of the Middle Ages, though we might feel that Bakhtin's rather sweeping appraisal of this culture reduces it to type. In the next chapter we can see Chaucer complicating the confrontation between official and carnivalesque in ways ignored by Bakhtin.

6

Wives and Husbands

The previous two chapters have in a sense been leading up to this one, where I consider the best-known figure in the *Canterbury Tales* (her extended 'autobiographical' 'Prologue' is twice as long as the tale she tells) and one who has received added attention in recent years, given the growth of a feminist critique of Chaucer's work. The debate over the Wife of Bath is a controversial one; one of the earliest modern feminist discussions of her, in Arlyn Diamond's 'Chaucer's Women and Women's Chaucer', views her as Chaucer's perpetuation of a medieval anti-feminist tradition, a 'nightmare' figure 'compounded of masculine insecurities and female vices as seen by misogynists' in whom Diamond is unable to 'recognize myself, or the women I know, or have known in history'.[1] Others have passed over the Wife's self-confessed lechery, fickleness, and deceit with less concern, and indeed the essay immediately preceding Diamond's in *The Authority of Experience*, by Maureen Fries, contrasts the Wife of Bath's qualities with the weakness of Chaucer's Criseyde in saluting her robust assault on patriarchal institutions like the Church, so that here Chaucer does indeed create a 'truly practising feminist', in Fries's phrase.[2] Critics would now I think be more cautious about suggesting we have an either/ or choice in the matter; the Wife is partly an exemplification of medieval anti-feminism, partly a protest against it, partly a mouthpiece of carnivalesque play and opposition, partly a signal of the limits to the carnivalesque. Whether we can find any resolution to the struggle of forces that takes place in the 'field' of the Wife of Bath might now strike us, given what we have seen of Chaucer, as an unreasonable expectation.

Diamond need not be surprised that empirical evidence of the women she actually 'knows' does not substantiate Chaucer's picture of the Wife; as I remarked above, much of the Wife of

Bath's autobiography, though she claims in the opening line of her 'Prologue' to speak out of personal 'experience', comes straight out of previous texts. Thus, when she tells us that at the funeral of her fourth husband she was already casting an eye on the fifth (ll. 587–99), Chaucer takes this information (along with much else) from Eustache Deschamps's *Miroir de mariage*; when she tells us that after she had safely caught her rich old husbands there was no point in attempting to please them any more (ll. 204–6), Chaucer is repeating the complaint against wives in Deschamps and in St Jerome's 'Letter against Jovinian', the latter itself repeating the charges in Theophrastus' *Liber aureolus de nuptiis* (*Golden Book of Marriage*). We see immediately from reading these sources for the 'Prologue'[3] how medieval anti-feminism feeds off textual self-perpetuation; thus St Jerome feels no need to do any actual 'research' into women: he knows all about them already because he has the unimpeachable authority of Theophrastus to inform him. That anti-feminism flourished in its own cloistered world of the clerical text and that text's succession is not to limit its power or influence; such texts, or the attitudes they convey, would be paraded regularly from the pulpit, as the Wife knows too well. Indeed, her scorn is directed particularly at churchmen:

> ... no womman of no clerk is preysed.
> The clerk, whan he is oold, and may noght do
> Of Venus werkes worth his olde sho,
> Thanne sit he doun, and writ in his dotage
> That wommen kan nat kepe hir mariage!
>
> (ll. 706–10)

Earlier in her 'Prologue' she notes how different things would have been if women had had access to literary education:

> By God, if wommen hadde writen stories,
> As clerkes han withinne hire oratories,
> They wolde han writen of men moore wikkednesse
> Than al the mark of Adam may redresse.
>
> (ll. 693–6)

In the case of Criseyde, hounded, one might say, by a textual tradition also, we saw Chaucer's attempt at intervention; the Wife of Bath is an incarnation of the tradition she so justifiably assaults, a 'nightmare' perhaps, but one castigating, like Frankenstein's monster, her maker. This comes to a head in the climactic scene of her 'Prologue', where Jankyn sits down by the fire with his favourite reading matter, his book of wicked wives, and proceeds to goad Alisoun into her attack on it and him. Her final triumph over Jankyn,

> He yaf me al the bridel in myn hond,
> To han the governance of hous and lond,
> And of his tonge, and of his hond also;
> And made hym brenne his book anon right tho,

(ll. 813–16)

is the consummation of the complete gender-reversal the 'Prologue' moves towards, with the male shorn of all the traditional sources of his power, property, literacy, legal authority – an act little short of symbolic castration. This revenge-fantasy (a revenge on patriarchy fully deserved, in the eyes of many readers) is not, however, as straightforward as it looks, for the Wife's 'Prologue' then modulates into a final section which describes the marital harmony and seeming equality that prevailed after Jankyn's capitulation: 'After that day we hadden never debaat' (l. 822). Though some readers have taken this happy-ever-after scenario at face value, it is clear that the Wife's soothing picture of mutual kindness is no less a piece of romantic self-gratification than the fairy-tale that she goes on to tell; we hear nothing of Jankyn's view of this happy marriage, partly because he is already dead, presumably having found this regime rather less sustaining than his partner. Role-reversal is then maintained until the end of the 'Prologue': rather than an 'equal' marriage, we have a powerful older wife guarding over a docile young husband, patriarchy on the other foot, so to speak. By defamiliarizing the usual situation, Chaucer dramatically refocuses it.

Such role-reversal continues into the Tale the Wife tells. Here the situation of the lusty young knight in bed with the disgusting old crone is an inversion of the common fabliau situation (compare January and May's wedding night in the 'Merchant's Tale'), and this might lead male readers to take such a situation a little more to heart. Although the Tale ends with a magical transition into mutual bliss (not unlike the 'Prologue'), the wife snaps out of fantasy land in the last eight lines, back, we might claim, into the world of fourteenth-century socio-economic reality:

And thus they lyve unto hir lyves ende
In parfit joye; and Jhesu Crist us sende
Housbondes meeke, yonge, and fressh abedde,
And grace t'overbyde hem that we wedde;
And eek I praye Jhesu shorte hir lyves
Than noght wol be governed by hir wyves;
And olde and angry nygardes of dispence,
God sende hem soone verray pestilence!

(ll. 1257–64)

Her Tale of eventual marital happiness is set in Arthurian times, when there were fairies in the land but no friars (ll. 857–81), a society scoured of the clerical institution she so battles with in her 'Prologue'; in these last lines, however, we are back in the world of the 'Prologue', of the sexual battle, of money and the marriage-market. Here, her ideal partner is one we are again more familiar with from male stereotypes of female desirability, a union of sexual energy with passivity (mistress inside the bedroom, servant outside it): 'Housbondes meeke, yonge, and fressh abedde'. Her partner can 'get fresh', but only in the bedroom.

The 'Wife of Bath's Prologue' and her Tale then arise from the context of anti-feminism but founder on sheer oppositionality, in spite of the desire the Wife expresses, both in the account of her own 'experience' and in her choice of story, to get beyond two-party politics to a state of agreement and mutual exchange. If the Wife is too dubious a role-model to be accepted as a 'truly practising feminist', we can certainly see in her the cost and consequences of anti-feminism. If Chaucer is again giving us an emphatic deadlock, we can see just how obstructive this is. Images of a kind of stalemate predominate in the 'Prologue'; whatever her husbands give out, the Wife can return: 'I quitte hem word for word' (l. 422); 'he was quit, by God and Seint Joce! I I made hym of the same wode a croce' (ll. 483–4); 'in his owene grece I made hym frye' (l. 487). The only equality here, we might say, is the equality of revenge. That the Wife's behaviour, indeed her very identity as the *Wife* of Bath, is determined by what she opposes, that she is an effect of the master-term, patriarchy, is a theme forcefully maintained. Thus she tells us that she got her old husbands drunk, and was then able to gain advantage by accusing them next day of trotting out all the old anti-feminist clichés in their drunkenness; in fact, as she admits, 'al was fals' (l. 382) and she was putting words into their mouths.

But this strategy is again determined by an anti-feminism that would see all women as liars, adulterers, and so forth; in response to this the Wife practises a little reductiveness of her own and sees all men as anti-feminists.

If the Wife of Bath is seen as both a 'protest' against anti-feminism and an exemplification of it, then it seems she neatly embodies what Bakhtin has to say in *Rabelais and his World* about the 'complex and contradictory phenomenon' of woman in the 'Gallic tradition' of writing leading up to Rabelais, and by extension in medieval culture generally. In the 'popular comic tradition' which 'is in no way hostile to woman and does not approach her negatively',

> womanhood is shown in contrast to the limitations of her partner (husband, lover, or suitor); she is the foil to his avarice, jealousy, stupidity, hypocrisy, bigotry, sterile senility, false heroism, and abstract idealism. The woman of Gallic tradition is the bodily grave of man. She represents in person the undoing of pretentiousness, of all that is finished, completed, and exhausted. She is the inexhaustible vessel of conception, which dooms all that is old and termi-nated...she lifts her skirts and shows the parts through which everything passes (the underworld, the grave) and from which everything issues forth.[4]

Bakhtin then goes on to talk of the uncrowning of the old husband by a young wife who represents these things, in an analysis we used for the 'Miller's Tale' in the previous chapter. Medieval texts, however, often mingled this 'positive' image of woman in the comic tradition with an ascetic misogyny to produce the contradictory portrayal that the Wife of Bath might seem to illustrate. I have quoted Bakhtin at length above because it is tempting, at first sight, to see the lusty and 'comic' Wife in her vigorous anti-patriarchy as just such an embodiment of the carnivalesque undoing of man, whereas the limitations of this role, which I have tried to bring out in my discussion, are just as evident. The fact that she too is growing old (see especially her famous lament on this, ll. 469–79) and that we can surmise she is barren (in spite of her fondness for the divine injunction to 'wexe and multiplye', l. 28), all this sets limits to any symbolic import we might see in her as 'the principle that gives birth', in Bakhtin's phrase, however much she might be the 'bodily grave' of the old order. We saw in her a principle of repetition rather than regeneration; not so much an 'uncrowner' of the male order as a usurper of it.

If Bakhtin's two traditions of viewing woman are entwined in the Wife of Bath, it is fair to say that Chaucer investigates their relationship rather more thoroughly and subtly than Bakhtin himself does. The latter's appraisal of the role of woman in the carnivalesque amounts to little more than two pages in a book of nearly 500, and there seems little worry here that in Rabelais's *Gargantua and Pantagruel* itself – a book *par excellence* of male feasting, male joking, male company – women occupy such a marginal role. In upholding the celebratory aspect of woman's role in the carnivalesque, and seeing this as not hostile or negative, Bakhtin seems to forget that 'woman' may have other identities than that of being the earth-mother male uncrowner, and that to be buried beneath the numinously symbolic role of the 'womb' risks the loss of any historical identity other than that differential to the male. Woman becomes all in Bakhtin's pages, but she thereby becomes nothing, we might say. Chaucer, however, brings out forcefully the problematics of this position, and the crippling male-centredness of the role; moreover, in not allowing the Wife any full carnivalesque 'triumph', he shows himself attentive to the pervasive and deforming power of medieval anti-feminism, and sceptical of the possibility of release from it. In this he has alienated some critics who find that Chaucer does not do full justice to the actual influence and independence of individual women at the end of the Middle Ages, particular case-histories that feminist historians are increasingly concerned to uncover and to stress, and that may suggest the prescriptive element in Chaucer's arguably bleak outlook.

In spite, then, of the emphasis on 'play' in the Wife's 'Prologue', and on the fact that her favourite season of play is Lent – 'For evere yet I loved to be gay, I And for to walke in March, Averill, and May, (ll. 545–6) – the Wife represents not so much a pagan, naturalistic victory over Christian piety (which would reverse the situation in the 'Merchant's Tale') as an inability to find final freedom from it. The fact that she wants holy writ on her side (in her extreme interpretations of it at the beginning of her 'Prologue'), that she continues within the institution of Church matrimony and that she frequently shows herself to be affected by the 'official' morality rather than simply defying it ('Allas, allas! That evere love was synne!', l. 614): all this testifies to her desire for some religious sanctioning of the sexual urge, an accommodation we might label Christian sexuality (and one that, however much Chaucer might puzzle over it throughout his works, he nowhere shows is possible). The orthodox teaching of the medieval Church on sexuality is declared in the 'Parson's Tale', where marital sex is permissible for three reasons: procreation, the payment of the marriage debt (that is, fulfilment of the contract that neither partner 'hath power of his owene body'), and as a kind of safety-valve to avoid lechery elsewhere (938–9). What sex certainly is not for is 'amorous love', and it is this prohibition that prompts the Wife of Bath's lament above.

As I have remarked, it is only in the 'Miller's Tale' that we might see sexuality put to a 'laughing' and uncomplicated carnivalesque use, though this Tale raises again the problematic position of women in such a discourse. As many readers remark, the young wife is the only protagonist not to be punished at the end of the Tale, though we can hardly read this as endorsing her freedom in any proto-feminist sense. It may seem unlikely that we can explicate the 'Miller's Tale' by means of the Parson's, but a passage on the Fall from Eden in the latter acts as an interesting gloss on the former. At first, the Parson might seem to be resisting anti-feminism by regarding the Fall, as the fault not of Eve (as was customary: see the 'Man of Law's Tale', ll. 365–71, 'Wife of Bath's Prologue', ll. 714–20) but of Adam, 'by whom synne entred into this world'. It transpires, however, that Adam is at fault rather than Eve, because, as a man, he represents the 'reason', whereas Eve, representing 'the delit of the flessh', could hardly have been expected to resist temptation in any case (321–33). Woman is here excused, so to speak, but only as a being incapable of moral agency, and the same is true of the Alison of the 'Miller's Tale'. The imagery of young, 'innocent' animals with which she is invested (ll. 3233–70) suggests that she functions outside of a moral order which pertains only to men, as 'reasonable' beings; to be punished at least involves a recognition of this state of a moral responsibility, whereas to go 'free' implies a patronizing attitude to women as amoral agents on a par with children or animals. The argument will rage on as to how far Chaucer was 'ever ... wemenis [women's] frend' in Gavin Douglas's famous phrase in the Preface to his sixteenth-century translation of the *Aeneid*; but at least his attitude is far from one of patronizing rejection or even patronizing gallantry; for an example of the latter, compare C. S. Lewis's dismissal of Criseyde's intelligence (in his insistence on her childlike innocence of the machinations around her) in Chapter 4 of *The Allegory of Love* (1936), with the situation in the text itself, where Criseyde certainly exploits her sexuality to gain what advantage she can.

7

Law and Order

Everyone who has ever written on the 'age of Chaucer' has located the late fourteenth century as a time of political and social turbulence, with an unruly royal court, a difficult relation between Richard II and his parliaments, the Lollard movement against Church corruption, the discontent that led to the Peasants' Revolt of 1381 – a turbulence accompanied by the clamour of developing social groups, particularly the mercantile and commercial interests that feature so strongly in the composition of the Canterbury pilgrimage, and the increased 'visibility' of women in many areas of socio-political life. It has been something of a cliché in past writing on Chaucer to rehearse his relative indifference to the political events around him, but much recent criticism has insisted on seeing his work in a detailed social and historical context, notably Paul Strohm's *Social Chaucer* (1989). Strohm argues that the *Canterbury Tales* is very much a response to a new sense of the 'competing social interests' that constitute the history of the period, and that in this work we see the 'maintenance of social order ... on terms receptive to previously excluded or underacknowledged ranks and groups'.[1] The *Tales* are sensitive to fresh and more flexible models of governance and hierarchy required by changing social patterns, and in a sense they offer no less than a new definition of the State itself:

> the hospitality of Chaucer's 'framing fiction' to the varied styles and genres and forms in which his tellers express themselves, and to the ultimate irreconcilability of their voices, thus enables the perpetuation of a commonwealth of 'mixed style', with ultimately reassuring implications for the idea of the natural state as a socially heterogeneous body that recognizes the diverse interests and serves the collective good of all.[2]

Strohm's book ends on the assertion that Chaucer's work allows 'readers in posterity a continuing opportunity to refresh their own belief in social possibility';[3] whatever the turmoil in the world around him, the *Tales* show that 'competing voices can colonize a literary space and can proliferate within it without provoking chaos or ultimate rupture'.[4] There is dissension and argument between the pilgrims, but it is placated, and this commonwealth survives intact.

Strohm's views have been contested by other critics who see in them the survival (in a new guise) of older ways of thinking about the 'genial' Chaucer; thus Pearsall in his recent *Life* remarks 'I have to see Chaucer as much more alienated from his society than this, much more pessimistic, much less "responsible"'.[5] But it is fair to say that Strohm is aware of the self-interest and limits to social utility in the *Tales'* project. He admits its ideological base in terms of the assurance such a solution would provide to Chaucer's 'predominantly *gentil* public';[6] notions of hierarchy and even absolutism are not abandoned completely, but recur, for example, in the concluding 'Parson's Tale', a lengthy sermon on sin and penance that recommends a 'refeudalization of relations' and which is 'appropriate to the announcement of a more rigid, descending order' in social terms.[7] Moreover, the inability of the *Tales* to find any real participation for the peasant class, whose only representative on the pilgrimage is the silent and well-behaved Plowman (he has no tale, and his portrait in the 'General Prologue' is one of idealized serfdom), shows graphically the boundaries beyond which 'social Chaucer' cannot go. In Strohm's reading, then, we have an interesting case of Chaucer's work attempting to negotiate (or, if you prefer, coming unstuck in the negotiation of) disparate social models of traditional order and emergent demand; and such a position is in keeping with the constant sense of fetching-up against oppositions I have traced in Chaucer's work throughout this study.

The opposition between traditional order and its discontents is apparent in the 'General Prologue', and in the sequential structure of the pilgrim party. We open with the knight–squire–yeoman triad, presented as idealized types rather than individuals in a descending order of duty and service. This keynote of hierarchy and stability does not, however, survive for very long into the 'Prologue'; with the introduction of the clerical estate, the commercial and professional elements, and the guildsmen, we move into a world often governed by financial self-interest and with a corresponding interest in the self as individual rather than as type. With the Wife of Bath, who comes just about midway through the sequence, we have a figure who challenges on several counts the archaizing chivalric order with which the 'Prologue' opens; as a figure with specific individualizing traits (from 'biside Bathe', and 'somdel deef', ll. 445–6), as a businessperson, and as a woman (and traditionally, therefore, in the lowest category treated in 'estates literature', as Jill Mann has shown in *Chaucer and Medieval Estates Satire*, but here promoted up the order) she might seem to represent everything in the new world that feudal society repressed. If by the middle of the 'Prologue' we feel that the challenge to what seemed the original social agenda has been well and truly declared, it is no accident that the pilgrims immediately following the Wife – the Parson and his brother the Plowman – take us right back to a world of idealized pre-commercial virtue and Christian obedience, as if to staunch the tide of modernizing self-advancement that threatens to overtake the 'Prologue'. But this is a temporary respite; in the words of H. Marshall Leicester, Jr., whose work underwrites the above discussion of the 'Prologue', the final five pilgrims described after the Plowman give a sense of a 'uniformly wicked and worsening world' growing on us as the 'Prologue' reaches its end.[8]

What Leicester calls on many levels a 'disenchanted' picture of society is sealed in the last pilgrim to be described, and the 'darkest', the Pardoner, who adds to the recurring note of Church corruption a specifically unsettling sexual identity – 'I trowe he were a geldyng or a mare' (l. 691) – that contrasts with the patrilineal and masculinist Knight–Squire succession that opens the 'Prologue'. As Strohm remarks,[9] the Pardoner also comes nearest to inducing a breakdown of the pilgrim collective, by exploiting the tale-telling to his own financial gain and by almost provoking a rupture with the Host; the Knight, significantly, intervenes to restore order. And recently Lee Patterson in *Chaucer and the Subject of History* has seen in the 'Pardoner's Tale' a replaying of the Oedipal story whereby the threat of castration in the exchange between Host and Pardoner at the end of his Tale 'enacts masculinism's deepest fears'.[10]

That there are threats aplenty to patriarchal traditions of authority throughout the *Canterbury Tales* needs no further underlining. If the Knight–father opens the 'Prologue', he also closes it and opens the tale-telling, in that the 'cut' to choose the first speaker falls to him (l. 845). As we have seen, he also asserts his authority during the pilgrimage in the Pardoner–Host exchange, and in preventing the Monk from continuing with the 'hundred' tragedies he threatens to tell (ll. 1972, 2767–79). The *Tales* end with another father–narrator in the Parson, and the final 'Retraction' with a prayer to Him who 'lives and reigns with the Father and Holy Spirit' (1092). But Strohm's argument that the *Tales* are aware of the need for a less traditional model of authority is shown in the fact that the 'master' of the pilgrimage, the Host, has no inherent lordship but one that is voted for by the pilgrims themselves, by 'oon assent' ('General Prologue', l. 777); this reflects changing views on the State towards the end of the Middle Ages as 'natural rather than ordained' and hence 'more a product of human choice than providential ordinance'.[11] And, although the Host is keen to reiterate his authority as the 'Prologue' ends, reminding the pilgrims both night and morning of the penalty for disobeying him (the payment of all that the whole party spend 'by the weye', ll. 805–6, 833–4), once the drunken Miller intervenes after the Knight to insist on telling his tale in contravention of the Host's own planned order (ll. 3125–7), there is little that the Host can do. And, of course, the 'Miller's Tale' leads on to the revenge-telling of the 'Reeve's Tale', and that in turn to the Cook's. Where is 'law and order' by the end of the fourth tale, we may wonder?

Authority and order are then pushed and pulled about in the *Canterbury Tales*, never entirely abandoned, not exactly enforced. In the works he wrote before the *Tales*, Chaucer's awareness of conflict is less specifically social, and the arguably greater influence upon him at that period of writers like Dante and Boethius leads to a consideration of order in more philosophical and 'cosmic' terms. For example, throughout *Troilus and Criseyde* there is a keen attentiveness to 'the lawe of kynde' (I. 238) and its encounter with civil law; 'Ye folk a lawe han set in universe' the narrator says, addressing Venus in the Proem to Book III (l. 36), but the idealistic notion that such a law is indeed an agent of universal harmony that, for example, holds 'regne and hous in unitee' (III. 29) is disproved in the course of the poem. Not only can Venus' law lead to acts of lawlessness, as in Paris' abduction of Helen, but it can ultimately result in the division of both kingdom and house, as in Pandarus' final words on his niece: 'I hate, ywis, Cryseyde; (v. 1732). Arcite, in the 'Knight's Tale', originally written around the same time as *Troilus*, announces that

> Love is a gretter lawe, by my pan,
> Than may be yeve to any erthely man;
> And therfore positif lawe and swich decree
> Is broken al day for love in ech degree,

(ll. 1165–8)

a passage deriving from the famous lyric at the end of the third Book of Boethius – 'who to love can give a law? | Love unto itself is law' (ll. 47–8)[12] – where Orpheus' looking back on Eurydice indicates the human love of kind that will threaten not only civil order but celestial harmony itself. These issues are by no means laid to rest in the *Canterbury Tales*, as we have seen in preceding chapters, but there is no doubt that Chaucer in the *Tales* shows a new interest in infra-social questions of law and authority. In Strohm's eyes at least these show themselves tractable to a type of solution, whereas the earlier questions may become less prominent, if no less problematic.

8

'The Father of English Poetry'

Since in the 1990s ideas of 'Englishness' are such a prominent subject in academic writing, and since Chaucer and his work might at first sight seem highly likely to be requisitioned by a nationalist ideology, I shall conclude this book with a brief investigation of the currency of the above 'title', first bestowed on Chaucer in Dryden's 1700 Preface to his *Fables*. When in 1866 F. D. Maurice defended Chaucer from the charge of being a Wycliffite – 'he is not that. He is simply an Englishman. He hates Friars, because they are not English and not manly'[1] – he presented a Chaucer frequently found in Victorian writing, and one often designated by the interchangeable adjectives 'English', 'manly', and 'healthy'. A veritable paean to this Chaucer can be found in Matthew Browne's *Chaucer's England* (1869): 'his *Canterbury Tales* contain...more Englishness than any other poem in the language', an attitude that, for example, leads Browne to dismiss any influence the *Decameron* might have had on the *Tales*, on the grounds that the former work is 'evidently mediaeval-Italian, – cowardly, romantic, and thin'; had not its tellers actually run away from the plague rather than facing it four-square, as we can be sure Chaucer and his tellers would?[2] It is fair to say that this jingoism characterizes nineteenth-century views on Chaucer rather than popular writing on him of the twentieth. The English Chaucer very much survives into the later period, of course, but now transmuted from a loather of friars and foreigners into a less aggressive founder of the nation's literature and shaper of the nation's character: the voice of merry, rather than militant, England.

Alfred Noyes's two articles on Chaucer in the *Bookman* magazine (1929–30) are a classic example of nationalist appropriation, concerned to minimize his debt to foreign authors, concentrating primarily on the *Canterbury Tales* to the exclusion of the rest of the *œuvre*, and seeing Chaucer as founding the poetic line of Spenser, Shakespeare, Milton, Shelley, and Keats, on the one hand, and, through his talents of characterization, the novelistic line (commencing at Smollett), on the other. The *Tales'* 'General Prologue' is properly the prologue to the entire native tradition, or, in Noyes's words: 'it is a gracious act of the Muses that they should have set at the head of the long and glorious pageant of English literature, this many-coloured company of pilgrims, winding through the lanes of an English April, down to England's noblest shrine.'[3] It is interesting to speculate how far the founding moment of the 'Prologue' is responsible for the popularity of the pageant motif (and indeed the pageant-play) in presentations of English history and literature in the inter-war years; certainly the idea of a pervading Chaucerian fatherhood is a common one at the time. Thus Sir Arthur Quiller-Couch's second 'Gossip' on Chaucer: 'it has sometimes occurred to me to wonder, when people talk of Chaucer being so racily English, if England be not...the jolly land she is because our literature has kept her so constant to this good fellow's tradition – that the jolliness is actually Chaucer's aura inherited.'[4] It is not that Chaucer is English, but that England is Chaucerian, an understanding at the heart of G. K. Chesterton's *Chaucer* (1932), where Chesterton gets much typically and brilliantly paradoxical mileage out of presenting his subject as both the distillation of Englishness and the originator of it.

Many writers on Chaucer have, of course, taken an opposite view; not simply French, Italian, and American writers who wish to show that Chaucer is essentially French, Italian, or American, but writers with no interest in nationalistic dismemberment for whom Chaucer's importance lies precisely in his Europeanism. It is not merely this aspect of Chaucer's work (as in its debt to European sources) that has set limits, for all his 'Englishness', to his availability as a nationalist text, but also the difficulty of extracting from his work the type of purple patriotic passage that could make of Shakespeare, for example (with nuggets like John of Gaunt's speech on England in *Richard II* – 'this precious stone set in the silver sea', and so forth), the wartime 'voice' of England. Hence Chaucer is in fact surprisingly absent from the national propaganda of the twentieth century.

There is also not much doubt that over the last fifty years we have heard a lot less about Chaucer as the 'father of English poetry'. This is partly because the modernist onslaught on the native line conducted by Eliot and Pound attacked the stable rota of names of the type summoned by Noyes above, and introduced a much more cosmopolitan tradition that, paradoxically, could not recognize Chaucer's own cosmopolitanism; in my opinion the modernists tended to accept, at face value, the common valuation of Chaucer as the merry English bourgeois: 'the leisurely Chaucer', as Pound called him.[5] Or perhaps the glamour in modern eyes of his near-contemporary Dante simply occluded Chaucer. At any rate, the questioning of the canon resulted in the deposing of the 'father' of that canon, and such a label is not likely to be reinstated in these anti-canonical and anti-patriarchal times.

Today, however, to return to the beginning of this book, Chaucer has a reputation for internationalism and a truly international reputation, and one that will no doubt be abetted by the electronic editions of his work and computer images of entire Chaucerian manuscripts promised on CD-ROM in the near future. In 1900, on the quincentenary of Chaucer's death, the then Poet Laureate, Alfred Austin, unveiled a memorial window to him in Southwark Cathedral, and took the opportunity to salute the qualities of 'character and intellect' that have led to the English producing the 'greater number' of the 'greatest poets'.[6] If in the millenarian excitements of the year 2000 the sexcentenary is remembered, it is unlikely to result in a similar effusion, and certainly, in academic circles at least, the 'Chaucer window' people will be mindful of is likely to be that called up on a computer screen.

Notes

INTRODUCTION: THE CHAUCER BUSINESS

1. A. C. Spearing, *Chaucer: Troilus and Criseyde* (London, 1976), 7.
2. See C. D. Benson, 'Chaucer's Unfinished Pilgrimage', *Christianity and Literature*, 37 (1988), 7–22.
3. D. W. Robertson, Jr., *A Preface to Chaucer* (Princeton, 1962), 321.
4. G. L. Kittredge, *Chaucer and his Poetry* (Cambridge, Mass., 1915), 2.
5. N. Coghill, *Geoffrey Chaucer* (Writers and their Work; Harlow, 1956), 48.
6. P. Strohm, *Social Chaucer* (Cambridge, Mass.: 1989), p. xiii.

CHAPTER 1. LIFE, WORKS, REPUTATION

1. D. Pearsall, *The Life of Geoffrey Chaucer* (Oxford, 1992), 55.
2. M. Praz, 'Chaucer and the Great Italian Writers of the Trecento', in *The Flaming Heart: Essays on Crawshaw, Machiavelli, and Other Studies...* (1958; repr. New York, 1973), 83–4.
3. G. K. Chesterton, *Chaucer* (London, 1932), 208.
4. Pearsall, *Life*, 218.
5. *Athenaeum*, 29 Nov. 1873, p. 698.
6. F. J. Furnivall, *Trial-Forewords to My Parallel-Text Edition of Chaucer's Minor Poems* (Chaucer Society, 2nd. ser., 6; 1871, rpt. 1881), 142–3.
7. See P. R. Watts, 'The Strange Case of Geoffrey Chaucer and Cecilia Chaumpaigne', *Law Quarterly Review*, 63 (1947), 419–515; C. Cannon, '*Raptus* in the Chaumpaigne Release and a Newly Discovered Document Concerning the Life of Geoffrey Chaucer', *Speculum*, 68 (1993), 74–94.
8. Pearsall, *Life*, 180.
9. C. F. E. Spurgeon, *Five Hundred Years of Chaucer Criticism and Allusion 1357–1900* (3 vols.; Cambridge, 1925).
10. Quoted in ibid. ii, pt. 2, p. 124.
11. John Dryden, *The Poems and Fables*, ed. J. Kinsley (London, 1962), 528, 531, 533.

12. F. J. Furnivall, 'Recent Work at Chaucer', *Macmillan's Magazine*, 27 (Mar. 1873), 383.

CHAPTER 2. DREAMS, TEXTS, TRUTH

1. M. Ellmann, 'Blanche', in J. Hawthorn (ed.), *Criticism and Critical Theory* (London, 1984), 106.
2. See B. F. Huppé and D. W. Robertson, Jr., *Fruyt and Chaf: Studies in Chaucer's Allegories* (Princeton, 1963), 91–2.
3. S. Knight, *Geoffrey Chaucer* (Oxford, 1986), 8–15.
4. E. T. Hansen, *Chaucer and the Fictions of Gender* (Berkeley and Los Angeles, 1992), 86, 82.
5. See J. Ferster, *Chaucer on Interpretation* (Cambridge, 1985).

CHAPTER 3. SOCIETY, SEXUALITY, SPIRITUALITY

1. D. Aers, *Chaucer, Langland and the Creative Imagination* (London, 1980), 135.
2. C. Wood, *The Elements of Chaucer's Troilus* (Durham, NC, 1984).
3. See e.g. W. Wetherbee, *Chaucer and the Poets: An Essay on Troilus and Criseyde* (Ithaca, NY, 1984).
4. P. Elbow, *Oppositions in Chaucer* (Middletown, Conn., 1975).

CHAPTER 4. READERS, LISTENERS, AUDIENCE

1. For more on this, see 'Chaucer's Audience: A Symposium', *Chaucer Review*, 18 (1983), 137–81.
2. L. J. Kiser, *Telling Classical Tales: Chaucer and the Legend of Good Women* (Ithaca, NY, 1983), 94.
3. G. L. Kittredge, 'Chaucer's Discussion of Marriage', *Modern Philology*, 9 (1911–12), 435–67.

CHAPTER 5. NATURE, CULTURE, CARNIVAL

1. M. M. Bakhtin, *Rabelais and his World*, trans. H. Iswolsky (Bloomington, Ind., 1984), 96.
2. Ibid. 6.
3. For a full catalogue, see ibid. 73 ff.
4. Ibid, 95.

5. Ibid. 212.
6. Ibid. 82.
7. Ibid. 241.
8. Ibid. 95.
9. Ibid. 96.

CHAPTER 6. WIVES AND HUSBANDS

1. A. Diamond, 'Chaucer's Women and Women's Chaucer', in A. Diamond and L. R. Edwards (eds.), *The Authority of Experience: Essays in Feminist Criticism* (Amherst, Mass., 1977), 68.
2. M. Fries, ' "Slydynge of Corage": Chaucer's Criseyde as Feminist and Victim', in ibid. 59.
3. Extracts from them are conveniently collected in W. F. Bryan and G. Dempster (eds.), *Sources and Analogues of Chaucer's Canterbury Tales* (Chicago, 1941), 207–22.
4. M. M. Bakhtin, *Rabelais and his World*, trans. H. Iswolsky (Bloomington, Ind., 1984), 240–1.

CHAPTER 7. LAW AND ORDER

1. P. Strohm, *Social Chaucer* (Cambridge, Mass., 1989), 157.
2. Ibid. 168.
3. Ibid. 182.
4. Ibid. 166.
5. D. Pearsall, *The Life of Geoffrey Chaucer* (Oxford, 1992), 247 n.
6. Strohm, *Social Chaucer*, 157.
7. Ibid. 178–9.
8. H. M. Leicester, Jr., *The Disenchanted Self: Representing the Subject in the Canterbury Tales* (Berkeley and Los Angeles, 1990), 400.
9. Strohm, *Social Chaucer*, 155.
10. L. Patterson, *Chaucer and the Subject of History* (London, 1991), 397.
11. Strohm, *Social Chaucer*, 150.
12. Boethius, *The Consolation of Philosophy*, trans. V. E. Watts (Harmondsworth, 1969), 114.

CHAPTER 8. 'THE FATHER OF ENGLISH POETRY'

1. F. D. Maurice, *On the Representation and Education of the People*, quoted in C. F. E. Spurgeon, *Five Hundred Years of Chaucer Criticism and*

Allusion 1357–1900 (3 vols.; Cambridge, 1925), ii, pt. 3, p. 83.

2. M. Browne, *Chaucer's England* (2 vols.; London, 1869), i, 49–50, 86–7.
3. A. Noyes, 'Chaucer', pt. 1, *Bookman*, 76 (Apr.–Sept. 1929), 195.
4. Sir A. Quiller-Couch, 'A Gossip on Chaucer, 2', *Studies in Literature*, 2nd ser. (Cambridge, 1934), 225.
5. E. Pound, 'A Retrospect', in *Literary Essays*, ed. T. S. Eliot (London, 1960), 7.
6. Austin's speech is reported in 'Chaucer and St Saviour's, Southwark', *Literature*, 27 Oct. 1900, p. 313.

Glossary

blesse bliss
brenne burn

chese choose
croce cross

daswed dazed
dispence expenditure

eft-sones again, another time
ek also
eschue escape
everych each
everydel completely

fare (1) go; (2) behaviour
forthi therefore
freendes friends

glose (1) textual commentary; (2) use circumlocutions, fair words
grame sorrow
grece grease

hap good fortune
hardely certainly
hele well-being
hente seized
here her
highten are called
hooly wholly
hyre her

Iwis indeed

kynde nature

laudes early morning church-service
letten prevent
liste pleased
lith lie

lust delight

mark image
mis amiss
moot must

nyce foolish
nygardes misers
nylt will not

oratories chapels
other either
overbyde outlive

pan skull
parfit perfect
pletynge argument
pleyned lamented
prively secretly

quitte paid back

routhe pity

shende disgrace
sho shoe
solas pleasure
suffisaunce sufficiency

throng thrust
tweye two

vyrelayes variations of the roundel

waxen grown
wexe increase
wise way
wode wood
wrooth angry

yaf gave
ywis indeed
ympne hymn

Select Bibliography

EDITIONS OF CHAUCER

Modern Editions
The Riverside Chaucer, ed. L. D. Benson *et al.* (3rd edn., Oxford, 1988). The authoritative modern one-volume edition of Chaucer's work, with excellent notes and commentary.

Troilus and Criseyde, ed. B. A. Windeatt (London, 1984). Edition with extremely detailed textual and critical annotations, and a parallel text of the relevant parts of Boccaccio's *Filostrato*.

A Variorum Edition of the Works of Geoffrey Chaucer, ed. P. G. Ruggiers *et al.* (Norman, Ok.: 1979–). A monumental, multi-volume edition of Chaucer, still in progress, with exhaustive textual and critical commentary.

There are also several editions of Chaucer's shorter works, such as the *Book of the Duchess*, ed. H. Phillips (2nd edn., Durham, 1993), and the *House of Fame*, ed. N. Havely (Durham, 1994), both published in the Durham Medieval Texts series, as well as innumerable editions of individual Tales, of which the 'Selected Tales from Chaucer' series published by Cambridge University Press can be particularly recommended.

Older Editions Cited in the Text
The Works, 1532, of Geoffrey Chaucer: with Supplementary Material From the Editions of 1542, 1561, 1598 and 1602 (Menston, 1969).

The Canterbury Tales of Chaucer, ed. T. Tyrwhitt (5 vols.; London, 1775–8).

The Poetical Works of Geoffrey Chaucer, ed. R. Morris (6 vols.; London, 1866).

The Complete Works of Geoffrey Chaucer, ed. W. W. Skeat (7 vols.; Oxford, 1894–7).

The Student's Chaucer, ed. W. W. Skeat (Oxford, 1895).

The Text of the Canterbury Tales, ed. J. M. Manly and E. Rickert (8 vols.; Chicago, 1940).

The Works of Geoffrey Chaucer, ed. F. N. Robinson (2nd edn., London, 1957).

BIBLIOGRAPHY

Hammond, E. P., *Chaucer: A Bibliographical Manual* (New York, 1908).
Griffith, D. D., *Bibliography of Chaucer, 1908–53* (Seattle, 1955).
Crawford, W. R., *Bibliography of Chaucer, 1954–63* (Seattle, 1967).
Baird, L. Y., *Bibliography of Chaucer, 1964–73* (Boston, 1977).
——— and Schnuttgen, H., *Bibliography of Chaucer, 1974–85* (Hamden, Conn.: 1988).

Annual bibliographies covering recent years appear in both the *Chaucer Review* and *Studies in the Age of Chaucer*.

BIOGRAPHICAL AND CRITICAL STUDIES

Space will not allow reference to all the very able and useful works published on Chaucer. The following should therefore be regarded as the selection of a selection.

Aers, D., *Chaucer* (Brighton, 1986). A 'new reading' of Chaucer that stresses his engagement with the contradictions of medieval ideology.
——— *Chaucer, Langland and the Creative Imagination* (London, 1980). Sees both poets' work as challenging prevailing ideology, for example in Chaucer's questioning of medieval patriarchy.
Austin, A., Speech on Chaucer cited in 'Chaucer and St Saviour's, Southwark', *Literature*, 27 Oct. 1900, pp. 313–14.
Benson, C. D., 'Chaucer's Unfinished Pilgrimage', *Christianity and Literature*, 37 (1988), 7–22. Referred to in my Introduction.
Blake, N. F., *The Textual Tradition of the Canterbury Tales* (London, 1985). Describes the history of the establishing of the Chaucerian text, debating the relative value of the *Tales'* principle manuscript sources, the Ellesmere and Hengwrt MSS.
Boitani, P., *Chaucer and the Imaginary World of Fame* (Woodbridge, Suffolk, 1984). Valuably places the *House of Fame* within classical and medieval traditions of writing on 'fame'. Undervalues Chaucer's irony.
——— and Mann, J., eds., *The Cambridge Chaucer Companion* (Cambridge, 1986). Introductory essays on various aspects of Chaucer's work.
Brewer, D., *Chaucer: The Critical Heritage*, i. *1385–1837*; ii. *1837–1933* (London, 1978). Anthology of critical extracts recording Chaucer's reception through the centuries.
Browne, M., *Chaucer's England* (2 vols.; London, 1869).
Bryan, W. F., and Dempster, G., *Sources and Analogues of Chaucer's Canterbury Tales* (Chicago, 1941). Excerpts from classical and medieval

works that Chaucer drew on, or that offer similar models.

Burnley, D., *A Guide to Chaucer's Language* (Basingstoke, 1983). Standard account of the linguistic features of Chaucer's work in relation to contemporary varieties of Middle English.

Cannon, C., '*Raptus* in the Chaumpaigne Release and a Newly Discovered Document Concerning the Life of Geoffrey Chaucer', *Speculum*, 68 (1993), 74–94.

Chesterton, G. K., *Chaucer* (London, 1932). A witty and bravura performance. May say more about Chesterton than Chaucer.

Clemen, W., *Chaucer's Early Poetry*, trans. C. A. M. Sym (London, 1963). Introductory account of some of the pre-*Tales* poems; still useful.

Coghill, N., *Geoffrey Chaucer* (Writers and their Work; Harlow, 1956).

Crow, M. M., and Olson, C. C., *Chaucer Life-Records* (Oxford, 1966).

Curry, W. C., *Chaucer and the Mediaeval Sciences* (New York, 1926; rev. edn., 1960). Entertaining and still valuable account of subjects like medicine, astrology, and dream-lore that feature in Chaucer's work.

Delany, S., *Chaucer's House of Fame: The Poetics of Skeptical Fideism* (Chicago, 1972). Argues for Chaucer's scepticism about literature as a vehicle for authoritative moralizing (in distinction to D. W. Robertson's work); a forerunner of many modern studies attentive to Chaucer's questioning of medieval ideology.

Diamond, A., and Edwards, L. R. (eds.), *The Authority of Experience: Essays in Feminist Criticism* (Amherst, Mass., 1977). See my Chapter 6.

Dinshaw, C., *Chaucer's Sexual Poetics* (Madison, Wisc., 1989). The first full-length feminist study of Chaucer, and still the most sophisticated.

Donaldson, E. T., *Speaking of Chaucer* (London, 1970). Collection of Donaldson's urbane and often humorous lectures and essays on Chaucer from the 1950s and 1960s.

Elbow, P., *Oppositions in Chaucer* (Middletown, Conn., 1975).

Ellmann, M., 'Blanche', in J. Hawthorn (ed.), *Criticism and Critical Theory* (London, 1984). Brilliant Freudian reading of the *Book of the Duchess*.

Ferster, J., *Chaucer on Interpretation* (Cambridge, 1985). Explores the dialectic between interpreter and interpretation in Chaucer's work to refocus questions of personal identity, political power, and literary meaning.

Furnivall, F. J., 'Recent Work at Chaucer', *Macmillan's Magazine*, 27 (Mar. 1873), 383–93.

—— *Trial-Forewords to My Parallel-Text Edition of Chaucer's Minor Poems* (Chaucer Society, 2nd ser., no. 6; London, 1871, rpt. 1881).

Fyler, J. M., *Chaucer and Ovid* (New Haven, 1979). Illuminating discussion of several of Chaucer's poems that goes beyond the Ovidian context.

Godwin, W., *Life of Geoffrey Chaucer*... (2 vols.; London, 1803).

Gordon, I. L., *The Double Sorrow of Troilus: A Study of Ambiguities in Troilus and Criseyde* (Oxford, 1970). Attempt to reconcile the poem's transcendental imperatives with its recognition of human sexuality.

Hansen, E. T., *Chaucer and the Fictions of Gender* (Berkeley and Los Angeles, 1992). Challenges criticism that asserts Chaucer's feminist sympathies, reading his texts as a quest to re-establish patriarchal values.

Havely, N. (ed. and trans.) *Chaucer's Boccaccio* (Woodbridge, Suffolk, 1980). Complete English translation of the *Filostrato* and extracts from other works by Boccaccio that Chaucer drew on.

Huppé, B. F., and Robertson, D. W., Jr., *Fruyt and Chaf: Studies in Chaucer's Allegories* (Princeton, 1963). Application to Chaucer of an Augustinian reading theory that posits essential Christian truth beneath the text's rhetorical surface.

Jordan, R. M., *Chaucer's Poetics and the Modern Reader* (Berkeley and Los Angeles, 1987). Study of Chaucer's problematization of the roles of poetry and of the poet.

Kean, P. M., *Chaucer and the Making of English Poetry* (2 vols.; London, 1972). Comprehensive assessment of Chaucer's contribution to the English and European literary traditions which he inherited.

Kiser, L. J., *Telling Classical Tales: Chaucer and the Legend of Good Women* (Ithaca, NY, 1983). Explores Chaucer's ironizing of the exemplum form in his poem.

—— *Truth and Textuality in Chaucer's Poetry* (Hanover, NH, 1991). Examination concentrating on the pre-*Tales* poems, investigating Chaucer's scepticism about poetry's access to authoritative truth.

Kittredge, G. L., *Chaucer and his Poetry* (Cambridge, Mass., 1915).

—— 'Chaucer's Discussion of Marriage', *Modern Philology*, 9 (1911–12), 435–67. Discussed in my Chapter 4.

Knight, S., *Geoffrey Chaucer* (Oxford, 1986). Reading of Chaucer in a 'consciously socio-historical light', arguing for his work as a dramatization of medieval class struggles.

Kolve, V. A., *Chaucer and the Imagery of Narrative* (Stanford, Calif., 1984). Fascinating and copiously illustrated attempt to present the first five Tales in the context of medieval iconography and manuscript art.

Lawton, D., *Chaucer's Narrators* (Woodbridge, Suffolk, 1985). Study of Chaucer's narratorial voices that engages with stucturalist and post-structuralist criticism.

Leicester, H. M., Jr., *The Disenchanted Self: Representing the Subject in the Canterbury Tales* (Berkeley and Los Angeles, 1990). Reinvestigates narratorial voices in the *Tales* from a post-structuralist perspective that challenges traditional humanist ideas about character and identity, arguing that Chaucer's work itself dramatizes the way the human subject is constituted by linguistic and other discourses.

Lounsbury, T. R., *Studies in Chaucer, his Life and Writings* (3 vols.; London, 1892). Magisterial and witty survey still valuable today, especially in its section on 'the Chaucer legend' (vol. i).

Mann, J., *Chaucer and Medieval Estates Satire* (Cambridge, 1973). Relates the figures of the 'General Prologue' to the established conventions of medieval 'social-classes' literature.

—— *Geoffrey Chaucer* (Hemel Hempstead, 1991). One of the Harvester/ Wheatsheaf 'Feminist Readings' series.

Martin, P., *Chaucer's Women: Nuns, Wives and Amazons* (Basingstoke, 1990). Feminist study. Like the previous entry, more conservative in its theoretical approach than either Dinshaw or Hansen.

Miller, R. P., *Chaucer: Sources and Backgrounds* (New York, 1977). Anthology of a range of classical and medieval texts that informed Chaucer's work.

Minnis, A. J., *Chaucer and Pagan Antiquity* (Woodbridge, Suffolk, 1982). Illuminating investigation of Chaucer's treatment of the pagan world in *Troilus* and the 'Knight's Tale'.

Muscatine, C., *Chaucer and the French Tradition* (Berkeley and Los Angeles, 1957). Seminal and still indispensable discussion of Chaucer's French literary heritage.

Nicolas, H., 'Life' of Chaucer, in *Chaucer's Romaunt of the Rose, Troilus and Creseide, and the Minor Poems . . .* , i (London, 1846).

North, J. D., *Chaucer's Universe* (Oxford, 1988). Exhaustive study of Chaucer's use of astronomy and astrology.

Noyes, A., 'Chaucer', pt. 1, *Bookman*, 76 (Apr.–Sept. 1929), 191–5; pt. 2, *Bookman* 78 (Apr.–Sept. 1930), 216-18.

Patterson, L., *Chaucer and the Subject of History* (London, 1991). Reads Chaucer's work as a complex struggle between the proclamation of individuality and an acknowledgement of socio-historical determinants on the individual subject.

—— *Negotiating the Past: the Historical Understanding of Medieval Literature* (Madison, Wisc., 1987). Discusses the (unacknowledged) political agenda of some important modern schools of Chaucerian exegesis.

Pearsall, D., *The Canterbury Tales* (London, 1985). Excellent summary of the critical debate in relation to each of the *Tales* and the work as a whole.

—— *The Life of Geoffrey Chaucer* (Oxford, 1992). Recent and reliable biography.

Praz, M., 'Chaucer and the Great Italian Writers of the Trecento', in *The Flaming Heart: Essays on Crawshaw, Machiavelli, and Other Studies . . .* (1958; repr. New York, 1973), 29–89.

Quiller-Couch, A., ' A Gossip on Chaucer, 2', *Studies in Literature*, 2nd ser. (Cambridge, 1934), 213–32.

Robertson, D. W., Jr., *A Preface to Chaucer* (Princeton, 1962). See discussion in my Introduction.

Rowland, B., *Companion to Chaucer Studies* (Toronto, 1968; rev. edn., 1979). Series of introductory articles.

Spearing, A. C., *Chaucer: Troilus and Criseyde* (London, 1976). Short but searching introduction to the poem.

Spurgeon, C. F. E., *Five Hundred Years of Chaucer Criticism and Allusion 1357–1900* (3 vols.; Cambridge, 1925). Enormous compilation of a vast range of references to Chaucer.

Strohm, P., *Social Chaucer* (Cambridge, Mass., 1989). Sees Chaucer's work as alive to the emerging social demands of his period, and as trying to accommodate them in a new model of community.

Watts, P. R., 'The Strange Case of Geoffrey Chaucer and Cecilia Chaumpaigne', *Law Quarterly Review*, 63 (1947), 491–515. An early examination of the case by a legal historian.

Wetherbee, W., *Chaucer and the Poets: An Essay on Troilus and Criseyde* (Ithaca, NY, 1984). Traces Chaucer's debt to classical poets and to Dante in reading *Troilus* as a quest to escape the corruptions of sexuality into spiritual transcendence.

Windeatt, B. A., *Chaucer's Dream Poetry: Sources and Analogues* (Woodbridge, Suffolk, 1982). Models or parallels behind Chaucer's dream-visions (including Machaut's *Judgement of the King of Bohemia*.

Wood, C., *The Elements of Chaucer's Troilus* (Durham, NC, 1984). A Robertsonian moralization on the dangers of the illicit love-making in Chaucer's poem.

In addition the Oxford Guides to Chaucer offer extremely useful commentaries on the works; see H. Cooper, *The Canterbury Tales* (1989), B. Windeatt, *Troilus and Criseyde* (1992), and A. J. Minnis *et al.*, *The Shorter Poems* (1995). The journal *Chaucer Review* and the yearbooks *Chaucer Yearbook* and *Studies in the Age of Chaucer* carry articles, reviews, and bibliographies principally relating to Chaucer. In recent years the journal *Exemplaria* has been to the fore in bringing modern literary theory to bear on Chaucer studies.

OTHER READING

Aers, D., *Community, Gender, and Individual Identity: English Writing, 1360–1430* (London, 1988).

Bakhtin, M. M., *Rabelais and his World*, trans. H. Iswolsky (Bloomington, Ind., 1984).

—— *Problems of Dostoevsky's Poetics*, ed. and trans. C. Emerson (Manchester, 1984).

Boase, R., *The Origin and Meaning of Courtly Love* (Manchester, 1977).

Boethius, *The Consolation of Philosophy*, trans. V. E. Watts (Harmondsworth, 1969).

Brewer, D., *English Gothic Literature* (London, 1983).

Brooke, C. N. L., *The Medieval Idea of Marriage* (Oxford, 1989).

Burrow, J. A., *Medieval Writers and their Work: Middle English Literature and its Background 1100–1500* (Oxford, 1982).

—— *Ricardian Poetry: Chaucer, Gower, Langland and the 'Gawain' Poet* (London, 1971).

Dante Alighieri, *The Divine Comedy*, trans. J. D. Sinclair (3 vols.; 1939; repr. London, 1971).

—— *Hell*, trans. S. Ellis (London, 1994).

—— *La vita nuova*, trans. B. Reynolds (Harmondsworth, 1969).

De Lorris, G. and De Meun, J., *The Romance of the Rose*, trans. F. Horgan (Oxford, 1994).

Douglas, G., trans., *Virgil's Aeneid*, ed. D. F. C. Coldwell (4 vols.; Edinburgh, 1957–64).

Dryden, J., *The Poems and Fables*, ed. J. Kinsley (London, 1962).

Gordon, R. K., trans., *The Story of Troilus: As Told by Benoît de Sainte-Maure, Giovanni Boccaccio...Geoffrey Chaucer and Robert Henryson* (London, 1934).

Hoccleve, T., *The Regement of Princes...*, ed. F. J. Furnivall (Early English Text Society, extra ser., 72, London, 1897).

Kelly, H. A., *Love and Marriage in the Age of Chaucer* (Ithaca, NY, 1975).

Lewis, C. S., *The Allegory of Love: A Study in Medieval Tradition* (Oxford, 1936).

Muscatine, C., *Poetry and Crisis in the Age of Chaucer* (Notre Dame, Ind., 1972).

Newman, F. X. (ed.), *The Meaning of Courtly Love* (Albany, NY, 1968).

Ovid, *Heroides and Amores*, trans. G. Showerman (London, 1914).

Pound, E., 'A Retrospect', *Literary Essays*, ed. T. S. Eliot (London, 1960), 3–14.

Rabelais, F., *The Histories of Gargantua and Pantagruel*, trans. J. M. Cohen (Harmondsworth, 1955).

Salter, E., *English and International: Studies in the Literature, Art and Patronage of Medieval England*, ed. D. Pearsall and N. Zeeman (Cambridge, 1988).

—— *Fourteenth-Century English Poetry: Contexts and Readings* (Oxford, 1983).

Spearing, A. C., *Medieval Dream-Poetry* (Cambridge, 1976).

Virgil, *Aeneid*, trans. H. R. Fairclough (2 vols.; 1918; rev. edn., London, 1934).

Index

Recent and Forthcoming Titles in the New Series of

WRITERS AND THEIR WORK

WRITERS AND THEIR WORK

TITLES IN PREPARATION

Title	Author
Peter Ackroyd	*Susana Onega*
Antony and Cleopatra	*Ken Parker*
Jane Austen	*Robert Clark*
Samuel Beckett	*Keir Elam*
William Blake	*John Beer*
Elizabeth Bowen	*Maud Ellmann*
Emily Brontë	*Stevie Davies*
A.S. Byatt	*Richard Todd*
Caryl Churchill	*Elaine Aston*
S.T. Coleridge	*Stephen Bygrave*
Crime Fiction	*Martin Priestman*
Charles Dickens	*Rod Mengham*
Carol Ann Duffy	*Deryn Rees Jones*
Daniel Defoe	*Jim Rigney*
George Eliot	*Josephine McDonagh*
E.M. Forster	*Nicholas Royle*
Brian Friel	*Geraldine Higgins*
Henry IV	*Peter Bogdanov*
Henrik Ibsen	*Sally Ledger*
Rudyard Kipling	*Jan Montefiore*
Franz Kafka	*Michael Wood*
John Keats	*Kelvin Everest*
Philip Larkin	*Laurence Lerner*
D.H. Lawrence	*Linda Ruth Williams*
Measure for Measure	*Kate Chedgzoy*
William Morris	*Anne Janowitz*
Brian Patten	*Linda Cookson*
Alexander Pope	*Pat Rogers*
Sylvia Plath	*Elizabeth Bronfen*
Richard II	*Margaret Healy*
Lord Rochester	*Peter Porter*
Romeo and Juliet	*Sasha Roberts*
Christina Rossetti	*Kathryn Burlinson*
Salman Rushdie	*Damian Grant*
Sir Walter Scott	*John Sutherland*
Stevie Smith	*Alison Light*
Wole Soyinka	*Mpalive Msiska*
Laurence Sterne	*Manfred Pfister*
Jonathan Swift	*Claude Rawson*
The Tempest	*Gordon McMullan*
Mary Wollstonecraft	*Jane Moore*
Evelyn Waugh	*Malcolm Bradbury*
John Webster	*Thomas Sorge*
Angus Wilson	*Peter Conradi*
William Wordsworth	*Nicholas Roe*
Working Class Fiction	*Ian Haywood*
W.B. Yeats	*Ed Larrissy*